RECLINING FIGURE

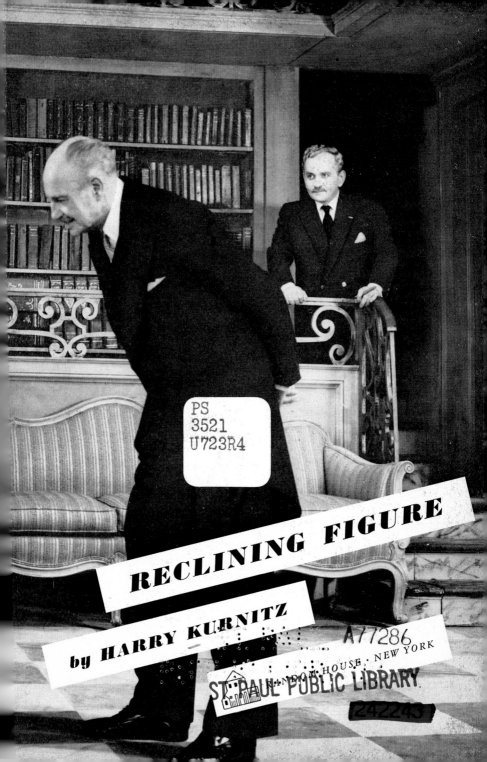

RECLINING FIGURE

by **HARRY KURNITZ**

RANDOM HOUSE · NEW YORK

To
ABE BURROWS
DIRECTOR, MIDWIFE, FRIEND

RECLINING FIGURE *was first presented by Martin Gabel and Henry M. Margolis (in association with Peter Cusick) at the Lyceum Theatre, New York City, on October 7, 1954, with the following cast*:

(In order of appearance)

WILLIAM	Foster Davis
SAMUEL ELLIS	Mike Wallace
CASS EDGERTON	Georgiann Johnson
LUCAS EDGERTON	Percy Waram
AGRAMONTE	Ralph Bunker
PAUL WELDON	Berry Kroeger
JONAS ASTORG	Martin Gabel
DENESCO	David Opatoshu
DR. HICKEY	Nehemiah Persoff
PROFESSOR JUMELLE	Alfred Hesse

Directed by Abe Burrows

Production designed and lighted by Frederick Fox

SCENES

All the action of the play takes place in the library of Lucas Edgerton's home in Pasadena, California.

ACT ONE
Morning.

ACT TWO
Evening, the same day.

ACT THREE
The following morning.

ACT ONE

ACT ONE

The library of LUCAS EDGERTON's *home in Pasadena, California, a few scant leagues from Oxnard. It is a large room, with masses of books. French doors at right lead to a terrace and the neighboring smog. Double doors at left lead to the rest of the house, which is a fine example of Southern California Gothic.*

A stairway rises from the center of the room, to the duplex living-quarter above. A balcony there leads to a bedroom.

Also at right, recessed in the wall, is a niche used for the exhibition of paintings. This is draped and has its own lighting system.

At left, sliding doors, now closed, give access to a huge vault.

The stage is empty at rise. WILLIAM, *the* EDGERTON *butler enters. He is a middle-aged Negro, of West Indian origin, with quite pronounced traces of it in his speech. He is followed by* SAMUEL ELLIS, *a young art dealer, carrying a fairly large painting wrapped in carton paper, tied with cord.* ELLIS *is in his early thirties, neatly dressed, at first glance a shade too tough a type for the business he is in.*

WILLIAM

In here, sir.

ELLIS

(*Looking back at the terrain he has covered*)
How big is this place?

WILLIAM

Mr. Edgerton likes to have a feeling of space.

ELLIS

He's got it. (*He starts working on the cord*) I'll get this unwrapped.

WILLIAM

May I do that for you, sir?

ELLIS

Thank you very much but—well, I'd rather do it myself.

WILLIAM

As you wish, sir.

ELLIS

I may seem like a nervous mother. This thing has just flown with me from Paris to Pasadena. I held it on my lap between planes. It shared my berth across the Atlantic.

WILLIAM

I'll tell Miss Edgerton you're here, sir.

RECLINING FIGURE

ELLIS

Miss Edgerton? I want to see Mr. Edgerton. I'm here on business.

WILLIAM

You'll have to see Miss Edgerton first. (ELLIS *shrugs, accepting this reluctantly*) May I get you a drink while you wait, sir?

ELLIS

Oh, no . . . too early.

WILLIAM

Perhaps just a glass of "Tingle?"

ELLIS

"Tingle?"

WILLIAM

Yes, sir. "Tingle." It's a soft drink.

ELLIS

Oh. The drink Mr. Edgerton makes—something like 7-Up, isn't it?

WILLIAM

(*Reproachfully*)

We don't think so, sir.

ELLIS

I'm sure it's a fine drink, but at the moment I don't care for any.

WILLIAM

(Pointedly)
Mr. Edgerton invented Tingle.

ELLIS

(It dawns on him, he moves to the bar)
Oh. You think?

WILLIAM

Quite a few gentlemen who come to sell Mr. Edgerton paintings drink nothing but Tingle.

(WILLIAM *goes out through the terrace.* ELLIS *pours himself some Tingle.* CASSY EDGERTON *enters from terrace with a clip board of insurance forms and pencil.* CASSY *is an extremely pretty, rather self-assured girl of twenty-five, twenty-seven, or thereabouts.)*

CASSY

Good morning, Mr. Ellis.

ELLIS

Oh, hello, Miss Edgerton. Nice to see you again.

CASSY

It's been a long time.

ELLIS

Quite a place you have here.

CASSY

What's that you're drinking?

ELLIS

Tingle.

CASSY

Did William say you had to drink it?

ELLIS

Oh, no, I always start the day with Tingle.
(*He drinks the Tingle and makes a terrible face.
He reaches for a recognizable bottle of Scotch
which he pours into the same glass and gulps.*)

CASSY

That's how *I* learned to drink Scotch.

ELLIS

(*Still suffering*)

What's in this?

CASSY

Oh, the formula is a trade secret.

ELLIS

I hope to God the Russians don't get it.

CASSY

Don't let my father hear you say that. (*Indicating the painting, still wrapped*) Is this it?

ELLIS

Yes.

CASSY

Will you unwrap it, please?

ELLIS

Miss Edgerton, isn't your father coming down?

CASSY

Yes, but I have to look at it first.

ELLIS

Why? Can't your father buy a picture on his own?

CASSY

The insurance company requires certain information while the painting is in our hands. So . . . if you'll unwrap it, I promise to take just a quick peek—won't hurt it at all.

> (ELLIS *takes off the wrapping, leaving the painting leaning against the sofa. It is a reclining nude partially draped, mostly where it counts, by Renoir and to the expert eye it is plainly of the rare, early period, 1875–1880.*)

ELLIS
(With a big gesture)

There it is.

CASSY
(Not terribly interested)

Will you put it over there, please? That's where my father likes to look at new paintings.

ELLIS

Over here? *(He takes painting to recessed easel)* How's that?

CASSY

Fine, thanks.

ELLIS
(He makes a trifling adjustment)

That all right?

CASSY

I think she's resting comfortably.

ELLIS

She looks wonderful, doesn't she?

CASSY
(She ignores the painting)

Number of paintings, one; type of painting, oil on canvas; name of painter, Pierre Renoir; date of painting . . . ?
(She looks up at him.)

9

RECLINING FIGURE

ELLIS

1878.

CASSY

Thanks.

ELLIS

(Starting to steam)

You're welcome.

CASSY

Title of painting?

ELLIS

It doesn't have a title.

CASSY

Well, how shall I describe it?

ELLIS

I don't care. . . . Call it "Ladies' Night in a Turkish Bath!" Miss Edgerton, how detached can you get? This is not an order of groceries.

CASSY

What do you expect me to do?

ELLIS

Say something. Say you hate it; say the girl is too fat —say *something*.

10

CASSY

It's a very beautiful painting, Mr. Ellis. I'm sorry if I seemed casual about it. But when you're Lucas Edgerton's daughter, you sort of take art for granted. Maybe that's not very healthy but that's how it is.

ELLIS

(Apologetically)

I'm sorry I pulled a knife on you. I should have realized that you probably already have a couple of Renoirs . . .

CASSY

Mr. Ellis, my father has forty-seven Renoirs.

ELLIS

(Awed)

Forty-seven!

CASSY

And sixty-one Cézannes . . . and thirty-nine Degas . . . and fifty-three Manets . . . and five Gauguins . . .

ELLIS

What's he got against Gauguin?

CASSY

Mr. Ellis, didn't you know about my father's collection?

ELLIS

(*dazed*)

I heard talk . . . but I didn't quite realize how . . . (*He looks around*) Well, you could never tell. I've been through the whole lower floor and I didn't even see a calendar on the walls.

CASSY

Everything is in the gallery.

ELLIS

Well, for all I care, he can keep his paintings locked in a safe. Miss Edgerton, your father is here, isn't he? He is expecting me? He got my cable?

CASSY

Yes, he's expecting you. Mr. Ellis, you know that when my father looks at the painting, he wants to do so in absolute silence.

ELLIS

Oh, I understand. I won't give him any sales talk. I'll just point out . . .

CASSY

(*flatly*)

You're not to speak to him.

ELLIS

If he sneezes, can I say *Gesundheit*?

12

CASSY

There are just a few more details of this insurance form—name of dealer, Jonas Astorg & Company . . .

ELLIS

Wait a minute. Hold it right there. Name of dealer: Samuel Ellis.

CASSY

Oh? Don't you still work for Astorg & Company?

ELLIS

I did work for Astorg. I no longer do.

CASSY

But I thought that when you acquired this picture you were working for Astorg.

ELLIS

When I acquired this picture I was working for Samuel Ellis. This is my picture. I'm an independent dealer. I have resigned from the firm of Jonas Astorg & Company.

CASSY

As of when?

ELLIS

As of—where the hell is your father?

RECLINING FIGURE

CASSY

(*With uplifted eyebrows at this sneak attack*)
I'll tell him you're here. (*She calls first to terrace*) William! (*Then to pantry*) William!

ELLIS

Miss Edgerton, I . . .

CASSY

Don't apologize. I think I'm lucky you haven't hit me. (WILLIAM *enters from pantry*) William, you ring Mr. Edgerton? (WILLIAM *nods*) And will you take Mr. Ellis' wrapping paper?
(WILLIAM *takes it and goes to pantry.*)

ELLIS

Miss Edgerton, I guess I'm overanxious, but you see I had a long 6,000 mile flight . . . this means a lot to me . . . It's really my first time at bat . . .
(EDGERTON *enters from bedroom on balcony.* CASSY *sees him but* ELLIS *doesn't.* EDGERTON *is a spare, crusty man of about sixty, eccentrically dressed.*)

CASSY

(*As* EDGERTON *comes down stairs*)
Well, Mister, step into the batter's box and start swinging—here comes the toughest pitcher in the league.

RECLINING FIGURE

ELLIS

Good morning, Mr. Edgerton . . . (EDGERTON *ignores him. Snaps on easel lights, crouches to examine the painting. After a moment,* ELLIS *cannot bear the suspense*) Mr. Edgerton, I'd like to point out . . . Oh, I'm sorry.

EDGERTON

For what?
(ELLIS *gestures to* CASSY.)

CASSY

Father, I told Mr. Ellis that you wanted absolute silence while you looked at the painting.

EDGERTON

Well, Cassy, that's true up to a point, but I wish you wouldn't make me look like some kind of damned eccentric. (*He looks at the painting from various angles. Then turns to* ELLIS) Say, you just left Paris. Tell me, why don't the French drink Tingle?

ELLIS
(*Startled*)

Don't they?

EDGERTON

No. Who the hell are they not to drink it?

15

ELLIS

Well, they're a nation of wine-drinkers.

EDGERTON

I know. They won't drink anything they can't trample first in their bare feet. They won't even try Tingle. You'd think our State Department would do something about that. In the old days, T.R. would have shoved it down their throats. (*He goes back to examining the painting, leaving* ELLIS *dangling. Then he turns to him again.*) Well . . .

ELLIS

(*Eagerly*)

Yes?

EDGERTON

So you've finally left Astorg, eh? .

ELLIS

(*Let down again*)

Yes, sir. You remember, that's what you once advised me to do.

EDGERTON

Advice is cheap. (*He examines the painting.* ELLIS *licks his lips nervously*) What did this cost you?

ELLIS

(*Instinctively*)

Fifty thousand dollars.

EDGERTON

You're a fool to tell a customer what you paid for a painting.

ELLIS

You asked me!

EDGERTON

Sure! But you didn't have to tell me. (*He returns to painting*) Say, where did you get fifty thousand dollars?

ELLIS

It wasn't easy, but I got it.

EDGERTON

Borrowed it, eh?

ELLIS

I was lucky. I found a wallet.

EDGERTON

(*He examines painting a moment then flips off the easel lights*)
Cassy! What time is lunch?

CASSY

Oh, in about an hour.

EDGERTON

(*Going to bar*)

Well, how about a drink? This is a great appetizer. A Rum-Tingle. (*Pours rum into two glasses, then grapefruit juice*) A jigger of Jamaica rum, a jigger of grapefruit juice. (*Pours Tingle from quart bottle*) Then fill to the brim with sparkling Tingle. (*Suddenly*) What are you asking for it?

ELLIS

For what?

EDGERTON

The painting.

ELLIS

Oh. (*He swallows. It is a big moment in his life*) Well, I think it's worth a hundred thousand dollars.

EDGERTON

(*Betraying no emotion*)

William! William!

WILLIAM

(*Entering on the double from pantry*)

Sir?

EDGERTON

William! Look at this lemon peel! It doesn't curl! I've told you over and over again, the lemon peel has to curl.

WILLIAM

(He peers at the suspect peel)
Yes, sir. It does curl, sir. . . .

EDGERTON

No, it's supposed to be a big winding curl. Give me a knife . . . *(He starts for the pantry)* I'll show you how to do it. It's got to look like a horse's neck.
(He goes out.)

WILLIAM

(Sadly)
This was a very stubborn lemon, sir.
(He follows EDGERTON *off.)*

ELLIS

(Summing up in a soliloquy)
Well, if a man wants curly lemon peel, why not? It makes sense. He's got plenty of Renoirs, but he hasn't got any curly lemon peel. He's Lucas Edgerton. Can't be anything wrong with him—I must be crazy.

CASSY

Mr. Ellis, let me explain about my father . . .

ELLIS

Please—I'd rather not know.

CASSY

I just want to tell you how his mind works.

ELLIS

I know how his mind works—sideways. (*Indicating painting*) That is not a Christmas card—it's a great artistic treasure. I show it to your father. He looks at it. He asks me how much do I want. I tell him one hundred thousand dollars. He makes me a counter-offer—a Rum-Tingle!

CASSY

He has his own way of doing things. He makes you earn your profit.

ELLIS

I don't mind suffering, if I could be sure he'd buy it.

CASSY

Well, you can't be sure of that.

ELLIS

What? He has to buy it.

CASSY

Suppose he doesn't?

ELLIS

But I got it for him!

CASSY

He didn't guarantee he'd buy it. (ELLIS *clutches his stomach, looking suddenly ill*) What's the matter?

ELLIS

Could I just now be getting air-sick?

CASSY

Whatever my father decides, it's a Renoir, and you'll sell it eventually.

ELLIS

Eventually is too late.

CASSY

Say, did you steal this painting?

ELLIS

You've inherited your father's wit.

CASSY

Well, you act like a man trying to unload a hot Renoir. I never thought of asking for proof of ownership.

ELLIS

Here. (*He takes receipt from his pocket, shows it to her*) Receipt for fifty thousand dollars. Twelve thousand in cash, and my personal check . . . (*This thought seems to sicken him)* For the balance. (*He sits, or falls, on the sofa*) Oh, my God!

CASSY

Is there anything wrong with the check?

ELLIS

There's nothing wrong with the check! In Paris it seemed like such a simple transaction . . . Maybe it was something in the air . . . something gay and foolish and tender—those lousy chestnuts in blossom! (*He feels his forehead*) Is it very warm in here?

CASSY

Not for people with money in the bank.

ELLIS

This was the only way I could break away from the Astorg Gallery and get out on my own. The minute I saw her, I knew she was Miss Liberty. I couldn't face going back to that plush, paneled super-market.

CASSY

I must say, the times I've seen you there, you seemed pretty miserable.

ELLIS

You mean you noticed me? I always thought you were looking right through me.

22

CASSY

Oh, I noticed you. You looked so sad in your little cutaway, and your cute striped pants. I thought of you as Sam, the Handsome Undertaker.

ELLIS

Well, Astorg likes the place to look like a funeral parlor.

CASSY

Maybe it's because the painters are all dead.

ELLIS

Maybe. Our sales talks certainly were all eulogies. Clichés followed each other like tracer bullets. Did you ever hear any of them?

CASSY

No, I was just an innocent bystander.

ELLIS

At Astorg & Company, a painting is never just a painting. It is either the final distillation of genius; or a monument to man's attainment of the unattainable; or, in special cases, it is the Master, with his brush dipped in immortality.

CASSY

Didn't you ever just call a painting a masterpiece?

23

ELLIS

When we had a sale.

CASSY

Well, if that's the way it was, I can't blame you for writing a bad check, to get out.

ELLIS

Not really a bad check. You see, I had some of the price in cash, but I couldn't swing it without writing a check for the balance. I thought I could rush out here, sell the painting and get back to New York before my check got there. It takes five days to clear, and—well, your father was always after me to get him something like this, and—well—you see what I had in mind?

CASSY

Grand larceny.

ELLIS

It's not grand larceny. I looked it up. It's obtaining money under false pretenses.

CASSY

Well, that makes it all right. And I'm sure you had a noble motive.

ELLIS

I had a motive. My own gallery.

RECLINING FIGURE

CASSY

(*This strikes a familiar chord*)
Ah, a little gallery . . .

ELLIS

Yes, with live painters and no striped pants. A place where a painter can get a break while he's still young enough to enjoy it. (*Pauses, look at her*) I know, you've heard this before.

CASSY

Yes, I have.

ELLIS

Have you ever heard of Harris Mitchell? He's a steamfitter. He paints on his day off. Ever hear of Nick Tully? He's a floorwalker . . . paints too, but only when he's not working at Bloomingdale's. And Joe Wilson, and Harry Stein, and Joe Cresta? These aren't Sunday painters. They're all talented artists who have to work at other jobs because they can't afford to paint. My gallery is going to support these guys. Give them a chance to paint, and give the public a chance to see what they paint.

CASSY

Say, that sounds like more fun than trading in masterpieces.

ELLIS

Sure. And you can help me. I've got to get your father down to business. (*Puts his arm around her*) He likes the painting; I know he does. He's got to buy it—*fast*.

CASSY

(*Thoughtfully*)
Yes, I see that.

ELLIS

(*Warmly, using both hands*)
It's more than making the sale now—it's meeting that damn check.

CASSY

I understand. You would do just about anything to sell the painting now, wouldn't you?

ELLIS

I knew you'd understand. Thanks.

CASSY

(*Pushing him away abruptly*)
If you're so anxious to sell your picture, why don't you try necking with my father?

ELLIS

I wasn't trying to use you. What kind of a guy do you think I am?

CASSY

You're a guy in trouble and you'll do anything to get out of it. All that big talk about a little gallery!

ELLIS

I should have known better than to talk to you about an idea.

CASSY

Mr. Ellis, a lot of young men have come here. Full of big ideas about art, science, lumber, Tingle—big, wonderful ideas, and how quickly they evaporate when my father waves *his* banner!

ELLIS

You're a sullen little cynic, aren't you?

CASSY

Oh, no. I believe in the big, wonderful ideas. I just don't believe in the small young men who have them.
(EDGERTON *enters from pantry, holding a long curl of lemon peel.*)

EDGERTON

Now, that's what I call a curl.
(*He goes to bar, and drops lemon peel into the two drinks he has prepared.*)

27

CASSY

Father, I'll be on the terrace.

EDGERTON

No, stay here, Cassy. I may need witnesses with this young pirate around. (*He sips one of the drinks*) Damn! That's good! (*He brings the other drink to* ELLIS) Here, son. Try this. (ELLIS *manfully takes a big drink*) Don't gulp it!

ELLIS
(*Shocked*)

Say—this is good.

EDGERTON

What'd I tell you? And you notice, there's none of that dark, bitter taste.

ELLIS

Yes—you can't taste the Tingle at all . . .

EDGERTON

You can't taste the *what*?

ELLIS

The rum.

EDGERTON

You said Tingle. I heard you.

RECLINING FIGURE

ELLIS

I said the rum.

EDGERTON

There's nothing wrong with my hearing.

ELLIS

Well, you didn't hear me when I said a hundred thousand dollars.

EDGERTON

You're changing the subject.

ELLIS

That's what you've been doing all morning.

EDGERTON

Well, I'm the customer, damn it.

ELLIS

You're not a customer—you're a collector. You know paintings. I shouldn't have to push you to make you buy a Renoir like this.

EDGERTON

A hundred thousand dollars doesn't grow on trees.

ELLIS

Well, if it comes to that, you don't have a Renoir bush in your backyard either.

29

RECLINING FIGURE

EDGERTON

(*He seems to be mulling over this thought*)
Bring it over here. Let me take a look at it in the daylight. Cassy, where's Agramonte?

CASSY

I phoned him an hour ago. He should be here soon.

EDGERTON

I'm anxious to know what he thinks of this.

ELLIS

(*Crossing, with painting*)
Why? Who is Agramonte?

EDGERTON

My expert. He's with the Santa Barbara Museum.

ELLIS

I had this expertized in Paris.

EDGERTON

I buy nothing without Agramonte's okay. How do I know it hasn't been damaged or retouched?

ELLIS

(*Putting painting against the urn, just inside terrace doors, He steps back*)
I would be willing to give you my personal guarantee.

EDGERTON

Your personal guarantee, eh? Is it as good as your personal check?

ELLIS

What do you mean?

CASSY

The F.B.I. uses *his* files.

EDGERTON

Don't be upset . . .

ELLIS

But . . . I don't understand.

EDGERTON

I called your bank and got your balance while I was curling the lemon peel. Don't worry about it. Some people might take advantage of that kind of information to squeeze a man . . . not me. (*Thoughtfully*) Still, a hundred thousand dollars . . . Better wait and see what Agramonte has to say.

ELLIS

Mr. Edgerton, if it's a question of price, I wouldn't mind a reasonable concession.

EDGERTON

What the hell kind of an art dealer are you anyway?
You take all the fun out of a deal. Fight, man, fight!

CASSY

Father, Mr. Ellis is unique—he doesn't really care
about money.

ELLIS

That's not true. It's just that I don't think it should be
the first consideration when it comes to selling paintings. In my new gallery if a man comes in who really
likes a painting, I won't let a few dollars stand in the
way of his having it.

EDGERTON

What new gallery is this?

ELLIS

Just an idea I've had for a long time, Mr. Edgerton.
Give the public a chance to know and love new painting.

EDGERTON

(*Wincing, as if struck a blow*)
The public? With my money?

ELLIS

The public drinks a lot of Tingle.

RECLINING FIGURE

EDGERTON

And that's all they're good for. The public! What the hell did the public ever do for painting or for any art? Show me where the public ever rushed around to help a painter with a new idea . . . or a musician . . . or a writer . . . Where was the public when Renoir was starving? Or when Van Gogh was going crazy from neglect? The public keeps its head buried in a comic book. The public!

ELLIS

Even if you're right, I've still got to try my kind of a gallery, and I've got a hunch that it will work.

EDGERTON

If it's one thing I am, I'm tolerant of young people and idle dreamers. I know what you feel and I understand. And I'm going to tell you something—*forget it*.

ELLIS

But, Mr. Edgerton . . .

EDGERTON

I said forget it. You won't have time for that kind of nonsense now. You'll be working for me.

ELLIS

Me? Working for you?

EDGERTON

Sure, and I've got a lot for you to do. There's a big sale of paintings coming up soon in Brussels. You'll represent me there. And you'll clean up in commissions.

ELLIS

It sounds . . . well . . . pretty wonderful, Mr. Edgerton, but, after all, Mr. Astorg is your dealer.

EDGERTON

Forget about Jonas Astorg. Hell, I invented him just like he was a soft drink. And now I'm just one of his clients. Can't even get him on the phone half the time. From now on I use nobody unless he is my own personal art dealer, and I think you'll fit the bill. This isn't snap judgment—I've had my eye on you for a long time. (ED-GERTON *studies* ELLIS) What's bothering you—ethics?

ELLIS

Well, yes. Maybe it sounds funny, after my quitting Astorg to bring you this picture but I never had any idea of taking your business away from him.

EDGERTON

What were you figuring to do—grab my money and run for the train?

ELLIS

Mr. Edgerton, why don't you just buy the painting? You don't want me. You're right—I'm an idle dreamer.

EDGERTON

Cut it out, son—start leveling with me.

ELLIS

All right. I left Astorg and stuck my neck out to get this picture because—well, because I like independence.

EDGERTON

I like independence, too. There's nothing I admire more than independence. But look, son, we can't *both* be independent.

ELLIS

(*Lost in admiration*)

Mr. Edgerton, maybe I'd better not try to explain any more. Just tell me one thing: am I to understand that if I don't become your personal art dealer, you won't buy my painting?

EDGERTON

Well, that's a harsh way of putting it.

ELLIS

Well . . . Miss Edgerton . . .

CASSY

Yes?

ELLIS

May I please have my wrapping paper?
(*He starts right, to the painting.*)

35

EDGERTON

What is he doing now?

CASSY

Father, it looks to me like you're being stood up to.

EDGERTON

Ridiculous! (*He turns on* ELLIS) What kind of a sneaky trick are you trying to pull off here?

ELLIS

I'm leaving. Got to find another customer for this painting and I'm rather pressed for time. So . . . (*To* CASSY) If you'll please get me my wrapping paper . . .

EDGERTON

You damn fool. You'll wind up in jail.

ELLIS

I've still got three-and-two-thirds days.

CASSY

I'll ask William where he put your wrapping paper. (*In pantry doorway*) You know, you look taller than when you came in.

(*She goes out.*)

RECLINING FIGURE

EDGERTON

What's she talking about? Why is everybody being so crazy? (ELLIS *picks up the painting*) Put that painting where it belongs.

ELLIS

Until you pay for it, it belongs with me.

EDGERTON

I'd like to sleep on it . . .

ELLIS

Oh, no. Not on my painting.
> (AGRAMONTE *enters. This is a curator type, if you ever saw one. He is neat and precise in all his movements, his speech is larded with the double-talk of his trade. He is about fifty, very dapper, wears dark glasses.*)

EDGERTON

(Leaping at the lifeline)
Agramonte! So you finally got here!

AGRAMONTE

Good morning, Mr. Edgerton. I'm sorry I was late.

EDGERTON

Never mind that now. Ellis, this is Mr. Agramonte.

37

AGRAMONTE

How do you do?

ELLIS

Nice to know you.

EDGERTON

(*With mock politeness*)
Well, Mr. Ellis, I am sure you won't mind if Mr. Agramonte has a look at your precious painting.

ELLIS

(*Responding in the same courtly manner*)
It would be a great honor, sir. (*Replaces painting*)
Here it is, Mr. Agramonte.

AGRAMONTE

(*Scurrying away from it*)
No. Please, no. Not yet. Don't show it to me.

ELLIS

You don't want to look at it?

AGRAMONTE

Of course. Most assuredly. Eventually.

ELLIS

Eventually again. It haunts me.

RECLINING FIGURE

AGRAMONTE

Mr. Ellis . . . (*He begins in a professorial manner*)
. . . I have just driven for two hours in the blazing
California sunshine. Can I immediately look at a fine,
sensitive Impressionist canvas? Would that be fair to
Renoir?

ELLIS

Would he have to know?

EDGERTON

Ellis, you keep out of this. Take your time, Agramonte. Don't let him rush you.

AGRAMONTE

Looking at a painting, Mr. Ellis, is one thing; viewing
a painting is quite another. You follow me?

ELLIS

(*Unhappily*)

I might as well—I've a feeling I'm not going anywhere.

AGRAMONTE

It isn't enough to see a painting, it must be observed.
When one looks, one must also contemplate. When I
scrutinize, I must also consider.

EDGERTON

(Cheerfully)

You're damn right.

AGRAMONTE

Let me go into Mr. Edgerton's great collection and browse among the early masters, gradually achieving clarity. Then at last my eye will be ready to judge the quality and the mood, the purity of line, the delicacy of color, the over-all tension, the dynamics of the canvas of Renoir, the master . . .

ELLIS

With his brush dipped in immortality.

AGRAMONTE

(Impressed)

Eh? That's very good. His brush dipped in immortality. Very good.

ELLIS

(With a low bow)

Be my guest.

EDGERTON

Well, while you're looking for all those dynamic delicacies, just remember what *I* want to know. Is it a Renoir—is it of the right year—is it in good condition . . . ?

ELLIS

Has it got calories?

EDGERTON

And see if it's been damaged or restored.

AGRAMONTE

Of course. May we go into the gallery now?

EDGERTON

(*Looking at his watch*)
Won't be open for a few seconds.

ELLIS

I'd like to see the collection, too.

EDGERTON

It's a private collection. Not a goddamn public gallery with a mass circulation. I show it to my friends, and my associates, not to outsiders.

ELLIS

I see what you mean.
(*A loud, electric alarm-type bell rings.*)

EDGERTON

(*Checking with his watch*)
Right on the button. The gallery is open.
(*He goes to the sliding doors and opens them, revealing a gleaming safe door.*)

41

ELLIS

(*The revelation stuns him*)
Oh, the bell was for . . .
(*Pointing to the vault.*)

EDGERTON

Sure. It's a time-lock. Built by the same firm that makes vaults for the mint and all the big banks. I lock it up at night and it stays locked until the time it's set for. Look at that door. Weighs nine tons—I can handle it with one finger.

ELLIS

A time-lock! (*He is still trying to assimilate this fresh lunacy*) But—suppose you want to look at a painting before the bell goes off?

EDGERTON

Why?

ELLIS

I don't know . . .
> (PAUL WELDON *enters, goes directly to the bar.*
> WELDON *is a cheerful, casual man of about forty-five, dressed in odd paint-flecked coat and trousers.*)

WELDON

Good morning. I see the piggy-bank is open.
(*He pours a drink of straight Scotch.*)

RECLINING FIGURE

EDGERTON

Be right with you, Agramonte.

AGRAMONTE

I'll be browsing.
> (*He goes to the vault.*)

EDGERTON

What have you got there?

WELDON

The little Degas I was cleaning up—the dancing girl.
Catch.
> (*He tosses an unframed small painting to* EDGER-
> TON, *who fields the chance awkwardly.*)

EDGERTON

Weldon, is that the way to treat a painting?

WELDON

Coming from you, sire, a fair question. The proper
way to treat a painting is to lock it up in a big vault,
thirty feet underground in steel and concrete. Walled
up where no unauthorized eye can fall on it. (*To* ELLIS)
Don't mind us. We're an old married couple.

43

EDGERTON

This is Sam Ellis. (*The introductions seem obligatory, so he performs them*) Paul Weldon. Works for me. Technician. Restorer.

WELDON

Handyman. (*They shake hands*) You're with Astorg, aren't you?

ELLIS

Not any more.

WELDON

Congratulations.

ELLIS

Are you the same Paul Weldon who . . .

WELDON

Yes, yes. I had a one-man show. Nineteen hundred and God knows when. That's me. Young discovery. Great expectations. Forty paintings. Sold a total of none.

ELLIS

No. You sold one. I bought it. Two old people on a bench in the flower market.

WELDON

Yes, the black shawls against the background of the bright blue flowers . . .

44

ELLIS

I still have it.

WELDON

I remember how hard I worked because the light was going fast. (*Back to reality*) I thought the Angelus would never ring today. The bell means two things to me—the gallery is open; and I can start drinking for the day.

EDGERTON

If you'd only stop drinking when the gallery closes.

WELDON

You're a bad influence. If I paid any attention to you I'd be sober all the time. Well, I'd better be getting down to Mamouth Cave. (*To* ELLIS) Be around for a while?

ELLIS

No, I just flew out to show Mr. Edgerton a painting.

EDGERTON

It's a new Renoir.

WELDON

Another Renoir. Let's see . . . this makes forty-eight —or an even one-third of a gross.

EDGERTON

If I buy it. Take a look at it.

45

WELDON

Always glad to look at one of your paintings while it's still out in the open air. Very soon this poor little painting . . .

(*He freezes as he sees the painting.*)

EDGERTON

What do you think of it? (WELDON *doesn't answer.* EDGERTON *is irritated*) Weldon!

WELDON

What?

EDGERTON

I asked you what you thought of it?

WELDON

Oh. It's good. Very good. (*To* ELLIS) A Renoir of this period is a pretty rare thing. How'd you happen to get it?

EDGERTON

Yes. How *did* you get it?

ELLIS

I was lucky. It was known to exist; but it had vanished—there wasn't a trace of it.

46

RECLINING FIGURE

WELDON

I know.

ELLIS

I was told that a Parisian family named Vernet first owned it. They were paint dealers. Renoir must have given it to them in exchange for paints or brushes—he was very poor then. They handed it down through the family and sort of kicked it around until it got lost.

EDGERTON

Damn fools. That's the French for you.

ELLIS

It was finally turned up by a small dealer, and—well, I got a tip on it.

WELDON

Very interesting. And now it's destined for the old Edgerton Mausoleum.
(*Indicating the vault.*)

EDGERTON

Go on—while you can still manage the stairs.

WELDON

You know, Renoir worked fifty years on the problem of the exact tint of light and the texture of air. Seems rather a pity, doesn't it?

(*He holds his nose and ducks down into the vault.* WILLIAM *enters from the double doors at left.*)

WILLIAM

Everyone is in here, Mr. Astorg.
(*He goes.*)
(ASTORG *enters. He is a man in his fifties, immaculately dressed or overdressed, a person of great confidence and flashy charm—and no integrity whatsoever. He has an indeterminate accent—could have originated anywhere—probably somewhere in middle Europe.*)

ASTORG

Quick, close the safe . . . here is Astorg. Ellis, what a charming surprise.

ELLIS

Hello, Mr. Astorg, I didn't expect to see you.

ASTORG

I know. Lucas, my dear old friend, how wonderful to see you.

EDGERTON

Astorg, my dear old friend, exactly what the hell are you doing here?

RECLINING FIGURE

ASTORG

I just happened to be passing by, so I thought I would drop in.

EDGERTON

I see, you left your office on 57th Street and took a walk by way of Pasadena?

ASTORG

It was a little out of my way . . . but what is that where friendship is concerned?

EDGERTON

One thing about having a friend like Astorg, you don't need an enemy.

ASTORG

Lucas, that's an old joke about Hungarians. I am now an American citizen.

EDGERTON

Well, if the White House is missing, I'll know where to look.

ASTORG

(*With a custom-tailored smile*)

Dear Lucas!

ELLIS

Mr. Astorg, did you get my cable?

ASTORG

Cable?

ELLIS

I sent it from Paris—about my going out on my own.

ASTORG

Oh, yes. Very nice cable. Very nice. Of course, you didn't tell me in the cable that you were coming directly here to Lucas Edgerton.

ELLIS

I meant to tell you . . .

ASTORG

I understand, my boy. You meant. Don't leave it worry you. Have you made your sale?

ELLIS

Well, practically.

ASTORG

Ah, that word "practically." I know it well. It is the epitaph of art dealers. Has any money changed hands?

ELLIS

Well, no. It seems a man named Agramonte has to see it.

50

ASTORG

Agramonte! Lucas, after all these years, must you still lean on Agramonte?

EDGERTON

Yes. He protects me against crooks like you.

ASTORG

I don't like that word, Lucas. Especially not from a man who has made ninety million dollars selling lemon-flavored Alka-Seltzer.

EDGERTON

Tingle has been damn good to you. You're in a sweat because Ellis is here. You can't stand new blood in the business.

ASTORG

I think new blood is charming. You know, Lucas, there is also new blood among collectors. Have you heard about Texas?

EDGERTON

It's in Rhode Island, isn't it?

ASTORG

In Texas they have a town, Dallas. It is exactly like Budapest. In Budapest everybody lies about how much money they've got, and in Dallas everybody lies about how much money they've got. Only in Dallas they are telling the truth.

EDGERTON

You're a natural for Texas. Someday they'll forget the Alamo and remember Astorg.

ASTORG

I must admit they worshiped me. In the beginning, I was worried. After all, these big sturdy pioneer people, would they do business with a foreigner? But it turned out fine. They thought I was from New England. (*Sees the painting and "points" like a setter*) Hmmm . . . is this the painting you've brought Mr. Edgerton? (*Deliberately*) Nice little painting.

EDGERTON

(*Wounded*)
What do you mean—nice little painting?

ASTORG

(*Baiting him*)
It has undoubted merit. Yes, very nice. Very pleasant little painting.

EDGERTON

Very pleasant! Suppose it was your painting?

ASTORG

Ah, in that case, an entirely different set of adjectives is involved. This? What can I say? It is not a monument to man's attainment of the unattainable. It's not the B-Minor Mass in a frame—it's nice.

EDGERTON

I know how you feel—one of your own juniors beating you to the punch on this.

ASTORG

You really like it?

EDGERTON

Yes, I like it. You know damn well I like it—and you like it too. This is going to be the greatest Renoir in my collection.

> (CASSY *comes in from pantry, followed by* WILLIAM *with the wrapping paper.* ASTORG *goes to her, his arms wide open.*)

ASTORG

Cassy, darling!

CASSY

Hello, Astorg!

ELLIS

I won't need that now.

> (WILLIAM *exits, with wrapping paper.*)

EDGERTON

Now don't get carried away.

CASSY

What's happened?

ASTORG

Your father has just bought a painting from this charming young man.

EDGERTON
(*Holding back the tide*)
Wait. Agramonte hasn't seen it. We haven't even talked money yet.

CASSY

So, the poor steamfitter will remain a steamfitter.

ELLIS

No, he'll be a full-time painter. And Bloomingdale's just lost a floorwalker.

CASSY

And I lost a bet with myself. Congratulations, Mr. Ellis.

ASTORG

Yes, congratulations, Ellis—and yet, condolences. Only a dealer's heart knows what it means to give up a painting for money. Remember, Ellis, how I cried when we sold that little Holbein—that radiant little girl? I loved her so. (*To* CASSY) Ask him. I cried like a baby.

ELLIS

Yes, he did cry. Real tears.

EDGERTON

Yes, it took a half-hour to dry the check.

ASTORG

I'm an artistic person. When I cry, I cry.

EDGERTON

Let me tell you one thing, Mr. Astorg. This is better than anything you've brought me in thirty years. This is one of the finest examples I've ever seen. Whether I buy it ir not. I can remember when you would have been scheming and plotting, burning up the wires, doing anything to get a canvas like this one.

CASSY

Father, why don't you stop needling Mr. Astorg? I think he's being very gracious about this.

ASTORG

I must admit I am behaving extremely well. (*Bows, kisses* CASSY's *hand*) Thank you, dear Cassy. I hope someday a brave knight will come to rescue you from this ogre's castle.

EDGERTON

Ha! Let him try it.

CASSY

Quiet, ogre.

ASTORG

You know, Ellis, I've been in love with this girl for twenty . . .

CASSY

Never mind my age—you'll scare off all the knights in the neighborhood. (*She goes to the bar, a little embarrassed*) How about a drink?

ASTORG

A little Scotch.

EDGERTON

Not me. I'll be going down to the gallery.

ASTORG

I want to propose a toast. This is going to be to you, Ellis.

ELLIS

That's very kind of you.

56

RECLINING FIGURE

ASTORG

(*Peers into his glass reflectively*)

It is always a sad and touching moment when one of the little fledglings leaves his nest to try his wings. To my new competitor.

EDGERTON

May he go broke!
(*He goes, to the vault.*)

CASSY

I admit he's rude. He's been spoiled—but he's been spoiled by art dealers.

ASTORG

Well . . . perhaps you are right.

CASSY

People who bow all the time make such good targets; he can't resist kicking them.

ASTORG

Now you tell me?

ELLIS

Mr. Astorg . . . I wonder if we might talk for a minute.

CASSY

I'm leaving. You can do this alone.

RECLINING FIGURE

ASTORG

As far as I am concerned, it is not necessary.

CASSY

No, I've got a lot of things to do. (*Pauses in vault doorway*) If one of you gets hurt, pour some Tingle on the open wound. It's great.
(*She goes to vault.*)

ASTORG

(*He goes to humidor on end-table, opens it and offers* ELLIS *a cigar*)
Cigar?

ELLIS

No, thanks.

ASTORG

(*Sniffs contemptuously at the cigars*)
I don't blame you. (*He closes the humidor and replaces it. Takes a cigar from his pocket for himself*) I gave Edgerton that humidor. You know what it cost? Twelve hundred dollars. It was made from a spice-chest that belonged to Anne of Cleves. Twelve hundred dollars! In it he keeps ten-cent cigars. Fantastic—these rich people. Wednesday I was in Detroit. A new customer. A man who has made millions of dollars manufacturing a plug or a brake or a switch—something foolish like

that. So—he invited me to lunch. *Lunch*? The first course was stewed grapefruit. Then a hamburger with cottage cheese and chopped nuts. The salad—an individual raw carrot. And for dessert, custard. Do you hear me, Ellis—*custard*. And such a man is buying Italian masterpieces of the sixteenth century. A custard-eater! Ah! Millionaires! Well, somebody has to be rich or we art dealers would be selling pictures to each other.

ELLIS

Mr. Astorg, I want to talk to you . . .

ASTORG

(Agreeably)

We're talking.

ELLIS

About coming out here, I want to explain . . .

ASTORG

Please. Don't explain. I understand.

ELLIS

Mr. Astorg, if you think I tricked you, let me split this deal with you.

ASTORG

My dear boy, I wouldn't dream of it. You found the painting, you bought it. I want you to sell it to Edgerton. I've helped you sell it to him.

59

ELLIS

It's very decent of you to feel that way.

ASTORG

Just one thing—I notice he seems to be interested in you. I do not intend to lose Edgerton as a client.

ELLIS

I don't want him. I've told him so.

ASTORG

I don't care what you want, or what you told him, he belongs to me. He is a monster, but he's mine.

ELLIS

All I want is a gallery of my own—my own kind of place. This Renoir is for sale—I'm not.

ASTORG

Ellis, I'm going to say something to you that I've never said to another human being—I believe you. You have the charming, impractical honesty of youth. You know, I was young once myself. Never as young as you, but young. I myself was a pioneer once. Yes, it's true. Today, with a painting by Renoir, Van Gogh, Cézanne, Gauguin, Seurat—you sit back and name your own price. It was different once. And in those days I invested my life and all I had in such paintings because I believed in it.

ELLIS

And what happened?

ASTORG

I could stand poverty . . . but I couldn't bear not to have money. (WELDON *comes from vault, and crosses to the bar*) Paul! Hello! Join us. We're discussing ideals.

WELDON

Ideals? Whose?

ASTORG

Paul is a man who has lost his faith. (WELDON *pours a drink*) We go back a long time, Weldon and I. We starved together in Paris. All we had was a little garret, a crust of bread, a little cheap wine. It was cold. There was no heat . . . You remember, Paul?

WELDON

Sure. Puccini. *La Bohème*, First Act. (*To* ELLIS) They want you in the lower depths.

ELLIS

Me? I thought Mr. Edgerton barred me.

61

WELDON

Well, Miss Edgerton has just unbarred you.

ASTORG

Ho-ho! Invited into the safe on your first visit. That's an hour.

ELLIS

Nonsense. If I don't come up in thirty days, please notify my family.
(*He goes to the vault.*)

WELDON

Nice boy.

ASTORG

Yes. I wonder how he developed so much character, working for me. (*He crosses to the painting*) Did you hear Edgerton? He said it was his finest Renoir.

WELDON

(*Joining him at painting*)
You know . . . I'd forgotten how good it was.

ASTORG

(*Respectfully*)
It is a masterpiece! (*Raises his glass to the painting*)
To a great Renoir!

RECLINING FIGURE

WELDON

A great Renoir? To the greatest Renoir in the whole goddamn world! And I ought to know—I painted it! *(They drink to it.)*

Curtain

ACT TWO

ACT TWO

Early the same evening.
The painting is on the floor, propped against the wall below the viewing recess. It is illuminated by a pair of photoflood lamps.

AGRAMONTE *is busy photographing the painting with a small camera fitted with a long telelens. After two snaps,* ASTORG *enters through the double doors, sees* AGRAMONTE *perched on the hassock, focusing. He poses with a prop smile, and* AGRAMONTE *unwittingly snaps him.*

ASTORG

Agramonte, if it comes out well, send me half a dozen.

AGRAMONTE

Mr. Astorg—if you please.

ASTORG

Why do you need a picture of a picture? It is already a picture.

AGRAMONTE

I find black-and-white close-ups an excellent method of studying the brush strokes. One's eye is then not confused by color.

RECLINING FIGURE

ASTORG

Brush-strokes! What a colossally meaningless absurdity! Agramonte, you know paintings. This is a great Renoir.

AGRAMONTE

I agree.

ASTORG

(*Pointing upstairs*)
You told that to the Führer?

AGRAMONTE

Mr. Astorg, if you don't mind, I don't like to discuss Mr. Edgerton in those terms.

ASTORG

Agramonte, you like it. You told him you like it. *He* likes it. Brush-strokes!

AGRAMONTE

Well, I don't quite understand it myself, but Mr. Edgerton insisted that I go through all the tests, make the complete survey.
(*He goes to the painting, reverses it, and snaps another photo.*)

ASTORG

What are you trying to find out now—if she has a mole on her back?

AGRAMONTE

This is a new test. (ASTORG *is instantly alert*) You see, the canvas is attached to the stretcher by means of nails. I photograph these areas, where the canvas is nailed, and then by studying the enlargements I can detect the strain.

ASTORG

Of course there is strain. The canvas has been attached maybe seventy-five years.

AGRAMONTE

Yes, but if this painting were not authentic there would be much less strain—and my photographs would show that.

ASTORG

I never heard of this test.

AGRAMONTE

I invented it.

ASTORG

(Bitterly)

Mr. Thomas Edison!
(WILLIAM *comes in from pantry.* AGRAMONTE *replaces the picture on the easel.*)

WILLIAM

Oh, Mr. Astorg . . .

RECLINING FIGURE

ASTORG

William, where is Mr. Weldon?

WILLIAM

I believe he is in his workshop. Mr. Astorg, there is a call for you. Long distance, from New York.

ASTORG

New York? Oh, my manager. Can I take it here?

WILLIAM

Yes, sir.
(*Indicates the phone. He goes to the bar.* AGRA-MONTE *gathers up the floorlights.*)

ASTORG

Will I disturb you, Agramonte?

AGRAMONTE

I'm going down to the darkroom.
(*He goes to the vault.*)

ASTORG
(*Into phone*)

Here is Astorg. Yes, yes, I'm ready to talk. Well, put him, put him. William, tell Mr. Weldon I'd like to talk to him. (WILLIAM *goes, by terrace doors*) Hello. Hello, Stanton. What do you want? Can't I leave the gallery for even a minute? Well, what is it? (*Listens*) Mr. Simmons—yes . . . (*Listens*) Well, if he wants the Manet portrait, sell it to him. (*Listens*) What do you mean, what should you charge him? You know our prices—how much can we get? (*Listens*) Thirty thousand, ha? I'll tell you what to do—ask seventy-five, and come down. But come down painfully. Mrs. Ziffer? Yes. She wants *what*? Michelangelo? For God's sake, where does she think I'm going to get it—off the ceiling in the Sistine Chapel? Tell her Michelangelo is *passé*. S*witc*h her over to that panel by Raphael. (*Listens, then impatiently*) All right, so it's a little dark. They've got electric lights in the house, haven't they? Now, Stanton, I don't know how long I'll be at Edgerton's yet, but from here I'm going to Houston, Texas. Ship me some paintings by air express right away to the Shamrock Hotel. What? Oh, send me the small Seurat—the Fantin-Latour—maybe the big Lautrec—oh, for Texas what difference does it make—send me altogether maybe a dozen assorted. (WELDON *comes in from terrace, goes to bar*) All right, Stanton. You'll hear from me. Goodbye. (*He hangs up, and quickly closes the vault door*) Drink. That's right, go ahead—drink. What do you care about the nail-holes!

WELDON

(*Politely*)

Nail-holes.

ASTORG

Your nail-holes. Agramonte is testing your nail-holes.

71

RECLINING FIGURE

WELDON

Well, then I'll just test *his* nail-holes. (*He finishes his drink*) It may be the liquor, but I could swear that we're standing here talking about nail-holes.

ASTORG

We are. Agramonte is photographing the nail-holes where the canvas is attached to the stretcher. He says that by enlarging the picture he can tell how long the painting has been there.

WELDON

Astorg, don't cast aspersions on my honor as a forger. First, tell me one thing. How did this painting turn up here?

ASTORG

You know how—Ellis brought it. What's the difference? What I want to know is what about those nail-holes?

WELDON

How did Ellis get the painting?

ASTORG

Who knows—beginner's luck. Paul, be sensible. Right now, Agramonte is testing those nail-holes.

72

WELDON

Didn't you once tell me that you had bought this painting back from the man you sold it to?

ASTORG

I tried to buy it back but it had disappeared.

WELDON

What happened to it?

ASTORG

A curious thing happened . . .

WELDON

I know—it was stolen by a ring of Algerian smugglers. You planted this for Ellis to find, didn't you?

ASTORG

All right, I did. I wanted this beautiful forgery to be in the Edgerton Collection. The boy won't get hurt. He's making a lot of money. But Edgerton . . . how nice for him that the first painting he buys from another dealer turns out to be a fake. This will keep him in his place and give my ulcer a rest.

WELDON

Where did you dig her up after all these years?

RECLINING FIGURE

ASTORG

A simple matter of logic. I asked myself, "Astorg, if you were a forgery, where would you be?" And the answer was easy. In a Roumanian art gallery. Remember Denesco? Georgi Denesco?

WELDON

Oh, a horror.

ASTORG

Exactly.

WELDON

He used to sell tourists Van Gogh's missing ear.

ASTORG

A very artistic person. I heard that he had this painting. And when I heard that Edgerton was interested in Ellis . . . and when I also heard that Ellis was looking for a Renoir for Edgerton, I said to myself, "Astorg, this is your chance to do a good deed."

WELDON

(*Indicating* EDGERTON's *chamber*)
He'll call out the F.B.I.

ASTORG

No. The publicity would be too embarrassing. Think how Pepsi-Cola would laugh.

74

RECLINING FIGURE

WELDON

You know, when I painted this I had a crazy notion it might wind up in the Louvre or in some other great gallery. But having it here is even better.

ASTORG

It's not in the collection yet. Paul, I've told you everything. Just tell me one little thing. What about those damn nail-holes?

WELDON

Forget about the nail-holes. They'll show plenty of strain. This is an eighty-year old canvas. I cleaned it and put it back with exactly the same nails in exactly the same place.

ASTORG

What about the other tests he's making? I've gone to a lot of trouble to arrange this barbecue for Edgerton. I wouldn't want anything to spoil it.

WELDON

Agramonte can test until he runs out of chemicals. I ground the colors by hand—they are exactly what Renoir himself used. I thought like Renoir—I worked like Renoir—I even grew a beard like Renoir.

(*His voice rises,* ASTORG *quiets him.*)

ASTORG

Paul, I want to apologize. I had forgotten you were such a genius. After all, it was fifteen years ago.

75

RECLINING FIGURE

WELDON

Seventeen years. I was young then, a promising artist. A golden future was ahead of me. And then I met you. And you showed me how to pick up a fast five thousand dollars.

ASTORG

Well, what was wrong with that? You were starving, and I needed money to get out of Europe. So we did it. It was an emergency. (*He glances up and sees* EDGERTON *coming from the bedroom.* WELDON *doesn't see this and* ASTORG *speaks loudly and ostentatiously*) Paul, I must say, I don't agree about Degas. (WELDON *looks startled, then sees* EDGERTON) To me, the essential quality of Degas is in the *faces* of his subjects . . .

EDGERTON

Say, Astorg haven't you gone home yet?

ASTORG

No, Lucas. I've invited myself for the week-end.

EDGERTON

I'm glad you did. I never would have thought of it. What are you all dressed up for?

ASTORG

Well, we are going to have dinner.

EDGERTON

I'll bet you dress for dinner on trains. Where's Ellis?

ASTORG

He's asleep.

EDGERTON

Asleep?

ASTORG

He's taking a nap in the dealer's wing. He was flying all night.

EDGERTON

Asleep! How can he sleep with a deal like this hanging fire? You'd think he had this sale all sewed up.

WELDON

Let him have a rest—he'll be able to stand more torture.

EDGERTON

(*Studying the painting*)
Look at that green in the background—the way the blue seems to shine through it. (*And catching himself*)
Not bad. Not bad at all.

ASTORG

Lucas, the boy can't hear. Let yourself go.

EDGERTON

That's painting, mister.

WELDON

Yes—it's quite a picture.

EDGERTON

Of course. This is Renoir.

WELDON

Why do you have to use the brand name? I say it's a painting; you say it's a Renoir. Wouldn't it mean as much to you if it wasn't a Renoir?

EDGERTON

How could it?

ASTORG

Paul, why don't we leave Lucas to enjoy the painting at leisure . . .

WELDON

I never could understand that attitude. Look (*He puts his hand over the signature*) I block out the signature. The rest of it is still great, isn't it?

EDGERTON

Take your hand off that!

RECLINING FIGURE

WELDON

Without the signature it doesn't mean a thing to you, does it? Your eye, your mind, your emotions—none of them matter.

ASTORG

Paul, such discussions prove nothing . . .

EDGERTON

They prove he don't know what the hell he's talking about. The signature is what makes it worth the money. Do you think I'm going to pay a hundred thousand dollars for a painting signed by you? Paul Weldon, Vat 69.

WELDON

I'll go change for dinner. I've got paint all over me.

EDGERTON

Stay the way you are. We don't have to go crazy because he's dressed up like an Indian with an oil well. Stay the way you are. Nobody dresses up around here
. . .

(*He stops as he sees* CASSY. *She enters from terrace, dressed in a beautiful gown. She enters briskly, then slows down as she becomes aware of the silence and the stares.*)

CASSY

Well—I'm a girl.

RECLINING FIGURE

EDGERTON

What is this tonight—the Captain's Dinner?

WELDON

Very sporty frock, Cassy.

ASTORG

Cassy, the dress is perfect. *Charmante. Très ravissante.*

CASSY

Hit me again.

WELDON

Now I really must get cleaned up.
(He crosses to bar, takes a whole bottle of Tingle, starts out.)

EDGERTON
(Surprised)

Tingle?

WELDON

Paint-remover!
(He goes.)

EDGERTON
(In a rage)

I tell you if he wasn't the best damn technician in the country . . .

CASSY

But he *is* the best damn technician in the country.

EDGERTON

That's the trouble, damn it. (*Looking over her dress*) Shouldn't there be more to it?

CASSY

(*Indicating painting*)
I'm wearing more than she is, and you're crazy about her.

EDGERTON

Well, I'm not her father. Say, what's making you so feminine and charming tonight?

CASSY

Feminine? Charming? Me?
(AGRAMONTE *has come from vault, examining a small microscope slide.*)

EDGERTON

What are you doing?

AGRAMONTE

Just looking . . .

EDGERTON

Looking at what?

AGRAMONTE

This paint.

EDGERTON

What about the paint?

AGRAMONTE

It seems to contain artificial resin.

EDGERTON

Artificial resin?

AGRAMONTE

Yes, phenol-formaldehyde. It's what makes oil-paints spread evenly and smoothly. It's in very common use. (*Shows slide to* EDGERTON) Very strange.

EDGERTON

If it's in very common use, why is it strange?

AGRAMONTE

Well, you see, sir, Renoir never used it in preparing his paints.

EDGERTON

Why not?

AGRAMONTE

Because, according to DeWilde's table, phenol-for-maldehyde wasn't invented until 1929, ten years after Renoir died.

RECLINING FIGURE

(He turns to the painting, unaware of the bomb-shell he has tossed into the group.)

EDGERTON

Now listen, Agramonte. Use your head, man. Renoir painted this in 1878. How the hell could he use a pigment that wasn't invented until 1929? Are you trying to tell me this is a fake?

AGRAMONTE

Oh, no, sir. It's perfectly possible that . . .

EDGERTON

(Ignoring him)

I own forty-seven Renoirs. I've been buying them for over thirty years. I know his work inside out. This is a great Renoir.

AGRAMONTE

I'm only saying . . .

EDGERTON

(Riding him down)

Don't tell me what you're saying. I'll tell *you* what you're saying. You're saying this is no good, that it's a forgery.

AGRAMONTE

No, sir. There may be a perfectly sound explanation of what I've told . . .

EDGERTON

(Shouting)

How the hell can there be an explanation? You call a painting like this a fake, and then you're going to talk your way out of it?

CASSY

Father, please listen to Mr. Agramonte.

EDGERTON

I *am* listening to him. Now you listen to me, Agramonte. Just because I hire you as my art expert, that doesn't give you the right to come in here and shoot your mouth off about a painting.

ASTORG

(Starts to rise)

Lucas, if I may offer a suggestion . . .

EDGERTON

You stay out of this, too. (ASTORG *subsides*) I don't want to hear any more fancy artistic talk. I know paintings because I buy paintings. And the reason I buy paintings is because I've got money. And the reason I've got money is because I've got more brains than all of 57th Street put together, including Carnegie Hall. Now let's have quiet so I can think.

RECLINING FIGURE

AGRAMONTE

Mr. Edgerton, if you'll listen to me for just a moment
. . .

EDGERTON

Where's Ellis? Wait till he walks in and hears all this.

CASSY

Father, I wouldn't . . .

EDGERTON

You wouldn't what?

CASSY

Why should Mr. Ellis be upset until you're sure . . . ?

EDGERTON

Why shouldn't he be upset? I'm upset.

CASSY

After all, he is our guest . . . he's had a long, tiring
flight. And he's been under a great nervous strain.

EDGERTON

Florence Nightingale! (*He goes to the easel*) Agramonte, where did you take the sample of the paint?

AGRAMONTE

(*Pointing to lower left corner*)
From that corner. And it's my opinion . . .

EDGERTON

Did you take a sample of the paint from any other part of the canvas?

AGRAMONTE

No, sir.

EDGERTON

All right, then. Now . . . isn't it possible that maybe just this corner of the painting was damaged, or faded, while it was in storage, or in shipment—and that modern paint was used in retouching?

AGRAMONTE

That's exactly what I've been trying to tell you.

EDGERTON

Well, why the hell didn't you speak up?

CASSY

He tried, Father, but the wind was against him.

ASTORG

Someone was shouting in here.

EDGERTON

All right, Agramonte. I've had enough of these damn tests. They're making me nervous.

86

AGRAMONTE

Yes, sir. I'm just waiting for some enlargements to dry. When I see those we won't need any further tests. They'll show exactly what this painting is, beyond the shadow of a doubt.

EDGERTON

Fine. (AGRAMONTE *starts to vault*) Enlargements? Of what?

AGRAMONTE

They show the brush-strokes in detail. They will tell us at once if the painting is in the natural hand of Renoir.

EDGERTON
(Intrigued)

Yeah?

AGRAMONTE

Oh, yes. Forgers nowadays are capable of many tricks but their brush-work invariably shows the strain of imitating another man's work.

EDGERTON

All right. You want to see this, Astorg?
(AGRAMONTE *goes to vault.*)

ASTORG

I think I'll take a walk in the grounds before dinner.
(*He goes hastily.*)

87

CASSY

(*As* EDGERTON *starts to the vault.*)
Wait a minute, Father. I want to talk to you.

EDGERTON

Come on—we can talk downstairs.

CASSY

Alone.

EDGERTON

Go ahead.

CASSY

What are your plans for Sam Ellis?

EDGERTON

Sam Ellis? If everything is all right, I'll buy his painting . . .

CASSY

And . . . ?

EDGERTON

And I'll give him a check . . .

CASSY

And?

EDGERTON

Well . . .

88

CASSY

That "well" is what worries me.

EDGERTON

Naturally, there are a few details I'll have to iron out with him.

CASSY

You're still set on having him work for you, aren't you? (*He looks at her blankly*) That's why you've been using these delaying tactics. Having Agramonte make every conceivable test . . .

EDGERTON

It's Agramonte's business to make tests. And it may be a good thing he's making this one.

CASSY

Let's just keep to you and Ellis. You still want him to be your personal art dealer, don't you?

EDGERTON

Well, what's wrong with that?

CASSY

But you heard him say he wouldn't do it.

EDGERTON

Yes, I heard him. I've heard it before. Ever hear of a man changing his mind?

CASSY

Sam Ellis won't.

EDGERTON

Well, if you're sure of that—no problem.

CASSY

Why don't you let him go? He wants to go to New York and open his own kind of art gallery.

EDGERTON

Cassy, leave it to me. It'll work out fine. I've had my eye on Ellis for a long time. Look in the file in my room. I know where he was born, who his parents were, where he went to school, even what marks he got. I need somebody like Ellis. There's one of the biggest collections of modern art in private hands in the whole world down in that vault, and by the time I'm through it'll be the biggest. Ellis is young enough to learn how I want things done. And he won't turn out like Astorg, with a lot of piddling little clients taking up his time. He'll represent me exclusively. Me—and nobody else.

CASSY

No, Father. Sam Ellis is for me—me and nobody else.

EDGERTON

Oh? When did all this happen?

RECLINING FIGURE

CASSY

It hasn't happened yet. But I think it will. I've been making some tests of my own.

EDGERTON

You think you know enough about him?

CASSY

I think so, but if there's anything else, I can look in your files.

EDGERTON

This morning I didn't think you were very keen on him.

CASSY

I wasn't. I was annoyed with him. Then you came, and he started talking to you, and I liked the way he talked to you.

EDGERTON

What was so nice about the way he talked to me? I thought he gave me a pretty bad time. He said a lot of rough things.

CASSY

To me it was pure poetry. I've had ideas about men before this—I'm old enough for that sort of thing, you know—and I'd bring them home and watch you make mince-meat out of them. And when I saw Battling Sam

Ellis stand up to you for two rounds, it made me want
to manage him for life.

EDGERTON

A hell of a reason to fall in love—just because a man
makes a bum out of your father.

CASSY

There were a few other reasons. Well, now you know
why I was so concerned about your plans for him. What
do you think?

EDGERTON

(*After a moment's thought, beaming*)
I like it.

CASSY

You do?

EDGERTON

I think it's great. It makes it perfect for everybody.
My own personal art dealer is my own personal son-in-
law.

CASSY

Oh, my God! You haven't understood one single word!

EDGERTON

What the hell is wrong with you? You want him,
don't you?

CASSY

Yes, I want him.

EDGERTON

All right, we've got him. I went to a hell of a lot of trouble to get him here. What do you want to do—let him walk out? (*She turns away from him, a frustrated gesture*) You turned out to be a girl after all. Use your head, Cassy. If you want him I'll get him for you.

CASSY

I'll get him for myself. I don't want a husband who has to be your own personal door-mat.

EDGERTON

He doesn't have to be a door-mat if he's got any guts.

CASSY

For years I've watched you break men down. Some pretty tough ones, too.

EDGERTON

Just a minute. I don't break men down. They break themselves down. They get close to the money and the main chance and it turns out that's what they want.

CASSY

Not my husband.

EDGERTON

Not your husband, eh? Well, I'd like to point out something—he's not your husband. All you've done so far is choose him. Are you sure he'll be delivered?

CASSY

I am.

EDGERTON

You've had too many charge accounts. (*He studies her*) I guess this new dress is the opening gun, eh? What's your next move—chloroform?

CASSY

No . . . I'll start him off on a martini. If that doesn't soften him up I'll do what any normal, healthy girl should do when she's in love—I'll propose to him.

EDGERTON

You'll *what*?

CASSY

All my life you've told me, "Cassy, decide what you want, make sure it's what you want, then *go get it*."

EDGERTON

(*A roar of outraged fatherhood*)
I didn't mean men! (*He heaves up a great sigh*) According to the rules of civilized warfare, somebody ought to warn Ellis.

94

RECLINING FIGURE

CASSY

No—I want to catch him off guard.

EDGERTON

All right, Cassy. Go ahead—take a crack at him. I won't interfere.

CASSY

You mean that?

EDGERTON

I won't have to. You admire Ellis because he wants to be on his own. Neither of you has ever been on your own. It can be tough going. When he has a chance to think, he won't want it.

CASSY

If he doesn't want that, then he doesn't want me.

EDGERTON

Well, I hope he does want you. (*He starts to the vault*) I'd better see how Agramonte is making out with his damned brush-strokes.

CASSY

Are you going to go—just like that?

EDGERTON

Like what?

CASSY

Well, the next time you see me, I might be engaged
. . . or something.

EDGERTON

Just be engaged. (*He kisses her on the forehead*)
Cassy, I wish I knew some father-of-the-bride talk.

ELLIS

(*Entering left, in shirt sleeves. He is groggy with sleep*)
God, how I slept. I meant to nap for twenty minutes
—that was four hours ago.

EDGERTON

Must have an easy conscience.
(CASSY *nudges him.*)

ELLIS

(*Looks at painting*)
Well, anyway, she's still here. I had a terrible dream.
The painting came to life. When I tried to sell it they
arrested me for white slavery.

EDGERTON

Arrested you, eh? That's very interesting. (CASSY
prods him in the ribs) Excuse me—I'll go down in the
vault with Agramonte. (*To* CASSY) If you have to dyna-
mite, don't blow up the house.
(*He goes to the vault.*)

RECLINING FIGURE

ELLIS

(*Staring after him*)

What was that?

CASSY

Oh, just something about Agramonte.

ELLIS

Is he still testing?

CASSY

He'll be finished very soon now.

ELLIS

All those tests. By now he must know the butter-fat content of my painting.

CASSY

Would you like a martini?

ELLIS

Before breakfast?

CASSY

Before dinner.

ELLIS

Oh . . . I guess I could use an eye-opener. (*He looks her over as she crosses to the bar*) Say, you look different. That's quite a . . .

97

CASSY

Oh, this is just an old house dress.

ELLIS

I didn't bring any dinner clothes. Is tonight some sort of occasion?

CASSY

Well, it's a little too soon to tell yet.

ELLIS

(Rises, takes drink from CASSY*)*
Thanks.
(He goes to the painting, stares at it.)

CASSY

Well, here's luck. *(He is absorbed in the painting)* Mr. Ellis.

ELLIS

(Coming out of it)
Oh, I'm sorry.

CASSY

It's all right. A girl gets used to not being noticed here when there's a painting on view. I've often thought of wearing a hand-carved frame, getting varnished all over and hanging from a hook on the wall.

ELLIS

It might brighten up the old place.

98

CASSY

She's unfair competition . . .

ELLIS
(*Looking at them both*)
Well, you're giving her a battle. Say, you are different.
This morning you were all . . . (*Makes an expressive
gesture*) . . . and now you're all . . . (*Makes another
gesture. Then puts his empty glass on bar*) Give me
another drink. Maybe I'll think of the right word.
(*She goes to bar and starts making another martini. During the following, she pours one jigger
after another into the pitcher, watching him all
the time.*)

CASSY

Mr. Ellis—where do you live in New York?

ELLIS

I've got an apartment on 55th Street.

CASSY
(*Still pouring*)
How big a place do you have?

ELLIS

Just a little apartment—one bedroom.

CASSY

That's enough.

99

ELLIS

It has been, so far.

CASSY

Do you live alone?

ELLIS

Yes. And that's exactly how I love a martini—thirty-three to one.

CASSY

Oh. I'm sorry. I was thinking of something else. I'll pour this out . . .

ELLIS

Just give me some straight Scotch. That's the only drink for a man who's waiting for Lucas Edgerton to buy a picture.

(*She pours the Scotch and brings it to him.*)

CASSY

You're anxious to get back to New York, aren't you? (*He nods*) Must have people waiting for you?

ELLIS

With open arms. (*She turns quickly*) All the receiving tellers of the Irving Trust Company. I've got to catch that rubber check on the first bounce.

CASSY

You'll get started on it right away, won't you? You won't let it get side-tracked?

ELLIS

I'll be rolling twenty-four hours after your father makes up his mind.

CASSY

Oh, don't worry about that—he made up his mind the moment he saw the picture.

ELLIS

Why has he had me hanging by my thumbs all day?

CASSY

He's been stalling on the chance that you might back down and go to work for him.

ELLIS

Work for him? He offered me that. I turned it down.

CASSY

It was a very flattering offer he made you.

ELLIS

I know. It was pretty tough turning it down. Frankly, I think I showed a hell of a lot of integrity.

CASSY

I think you were wonderful.

ELLIS

I wasn't bad, was I? Considering . . . (*Imitating Edgerton*) Ellis, forget your own gallery. Ellis, you're working for me. Ellis, roll over. Ellis, get your ball. Ellis, play dead. Ellis *drop* dead.

CASSY

You were scared, weren't you?

ELLIS

I felt like a guy in an *un*-fixed wrestling match.

CASSY

Well, you won—if you're tough enough to stick to what you said.
(*She sits beside him.*)

ELLIS

I'll stick to it. I'll show the old—(*Looks at her*)—the old gentleman.

CASSY

What if your money runs out?

ELLIS

That's a grim thought. Say, you're doing an Agramonte on me. You're testing.

CASSY

Maybe I am. You are a novelty.

ELLIS

You mean . . . sort of a one-headed art dealer.

CASSY

Well, let's say a scientific curiosity. And in the interests of science, I'm questioning you about your future plans.

ELLIS

I've told you all about my plans.

CASSY

Tell me again—slowly.

ELLIS

All right—once more, and listen. Me—open own gallery—New York City—me burn striped pants—me run gallery just the way goddamn please.

CASSY

You catchum squaw?

ELLIS

Catchum what? Squaw? Oh, that's a long way off. With a new gallery, and a flock of crazy new painters . . . all I need is a wife.

RECLINING FIGURE

CASSY

Well . . . I don't know . . . sometimes a wife . . . the right kind of wife—and I admit they're rare—can be . . . you know, a loyal, willing helpmate by your side, struggling with you every step of the way and never leaving your side even at the darkest moments.

ELLIS

That really sounds ghastly.

CASSY

I guess it does. But a wife *can* be an asset . . .

ELLIS

I suppose so. I imagine that one of these days I'll be thinking about it.

CASSY

Why don't you start now?

ELLIS

Start what?

CASSY

Thinking about it.

ELLIS

Now?

CASSY

Now.

ELLIS

Right now? (*She nods. They kiss, and break apart*) I didn't know I was such a fast worker.

CASSY

You had an awful lot of help.

ELLIS

(*He leaps to his feet*)
What am I doing? You're Lucas Edgerton's daughter!

CASSY

Did you think I was his son?

ELLIS

Lucas Edg——— The thought never entered my mind.

CASSY

It never enters anybody's mind. That's why I decided to take the law into my own hands.

ELLIS

(*It's all he can think of*)
But you're Lucas Edgerton's daughter.

CASSY

Don't keep saying that. I've heard it all my life. I grew up as the little jewel of the Edgerton Collection. I was being raised to be the keeper of the flame. I played with art books before I could read, and when I could read, I read art books. When other little girls were playing nasty games with other little boys I was curled up with DeWilde's Chronological Table of Pigments. I never did find out what those nasty games were.

ELLIS

I remember some of them.

CASSY

You do?

ELLIS

Yes . . . But just one thing . . .

CASSY

What?

ELLIS

Don't tell your father.
    (*He kisses her.*)

CASSY

    (*When they come out of it*)
I've already told my father.
    (*They kiss again.*)

ELLIS

You told your father? Lucas Edgerton? But . . . nothing happened until a minute ago. What could you tell him?

CASSY

I told him I thought you were very nice . . . honest
. . . very attractive, and . . . (*Bluntly*) Well, why do
you think I wore this dress?

ELLIS

I feel like a duck in a shooting gallery. What did your
father say?

CASSY

Well, you know, he wanted you, too.

ELLIS

What did you do—cut cards for me?

CASSY

No. He gave me first crack. He thinks he'll get you
eventually . . . that you won't be able to resist the
main chance.

ELLIS

That's why you were testing me, eh? Well, I don't
blame you. Sure I want the main chance. Who doesn't?
But to me, the main chance means a chance to do what
I've always wanted to do. I don't want to have to be
slippery. If I spend my life doing business with Astorg,
or your father, I'd have to be slippery—just to be so-
ciable. That's why I wrote a bad check in Paris, which is
the only crooked thing I've ever done—to keep from becoming a crook.

CASSY

Sam, you're a good boy.
(*They kiss.*)

ASTORG

(*Looming up in the terrace door, behind them*)
This is what I call salesmanship.
(*They separate hastily.*)

CASSY

Astorg, I'd better tell the cook you're staying for dinner.

ASTORG

The cook knows. I already gave her a bottle of "Arpege."

CASSY

That's probably in the gravy by now. Sam, why don't you finish dressing?

ELLIS

All right, dear.

ASTORG

Dear? This he never learned from me.

ELLIS

Modern methods, Astorg. Consumer resistance must be battered down by any means.

ASTORG

So, Cassy?

CASSY

Well, Astorg?

ASTORG

Cassy, I gave you your first bicycle. . . . It had belonged to the Archduke Rudolf, when he was a little boy. He later died at Mayerling.

CASSY

I remember you told me that when I was five years old. When I learned to read, I looked on the handlebars and it said "Made in Jersey City."

ASTORG

You see—that's an art dealer for you. That's why I don't like this tutti-frutti you are making with Ellis.

CASSY

What's wrong with Ellis?

ASTORG

Outside of one or two unusual art dealers, like myself —it's not for you, Cassy.

CASSY

Sam is different.

ASTORG

Different! In Budapest they have a saying, "Scratch an art dealer—and count your fingers."

CASSY

Astorg, Sam is not going to work for my father. He is going to be independent, in his own gallery. You are not losing my father as a client. Now how do you feel about Sam and me?

ASTORG

Like I always did: you were made for each other! I must think of a very special wedding gift for you. Ah! I have a silver tea service. Beautiful. It belonged to the Archduke Rudolf. (CASSY *goes to the vault*) This really did! (*He follows her to vault.*)

    (*From the left,* WILLIAM *ushers in* GREGORY DE-NESCO, *a dapper Roumanian in a suit of European cut. He carries a long, narrow paper tube, which he has tucked under his arm.*)

WILLIAM

If you'll wait here, sir, Mr. Ellis will be down in a moment.

    (DENESCO *nods without speaking, looks at the painting and around the room. On the end table he finds a cocktail glass, which he picks up and flicks with his finger. It doesn't ring. He gives a disgusted look, sits on the sofa.*)

RECLINING FIGURE

ELLIS

(As he enters)

You wanted to see me?

DENESCO

Mr. Ellis?

ELLIS

Yes.

DENESCO

My name is Denesco. Gregory Denesco. I live in Los Angeles and when I heard that you were in Pasadena . . .

ELLIS

How did you hear that?

DENESCO

News travels . . . in artistic matters. I am a sensitive person. I drove over here because I have something that will interest you, Mr. Ellis—a Renoir drawing.

ELLIS

I am interested in Renoir, but not particularly in drawings.

DENESCO

I understand. In my own palace, in Roumania, drawings were hung only in the servants' hall. But this is a very unusual drawing, Mr. Ellis. My brother, Georgi Denesco, who lives in Paris, sent it to me. He think this drawing will interest you.

ELLIS

Why should it?

DENESCO

It is of the same period as the painting you recently acquired.
(*He nods toward the easel.*)

ELLIS

Well, it doesn't interest me. (*Taking his arm, as if to escort him out*) Perhaps another time, Mr. . . . (*Tentatively*) Denesco?

DENESCO

Exactly. Denesco. You have a very good ear, Mr. Ellis. My drawing is so much like your great Renoir painting, Mr. Ellis, that frankly I would not like to see it fall into other hands. May I proceed?

ELLIS

Go on.

DENESCO

I thank you for your courtesy, Mr. Ellis. Basically, I am a connoisseur of fine things—(*With a shrug*)—life has made me a man who buys and sells.

RECLINING FIGURE

ELLIS

What makes this drawing so much like my Renoir?

DENESCO

Several things. (*He ticks them off*) They are both very beautiful; they are both reclining figures; they are of the same period—(*A pause, then lightly*)—and they are both beautiful forgeries.

ELLIS

That's not a very good joke—even in Roumanian. Now get the hell out of here.

DENESCO

I do not joke about forgery, Mr. Ellis. It is a serious subject; it must be treated with respect.

ELLIS

You call my painting a forgery once more and I'll break your crooked neck.

DENESCO

I am formerly Lieutenant Colonel in the Royal Roumanian Cavalry, Mr. Ellis. I mention this only so that you know that if I ignore your remark it is not cowardice.

ELLIS

Let me see that drawing. Come on, hand it over.

DENESCO

It would be wrong to show it to you in this frame of mind, Mr. Ellis. I am sorry this has so upset you.

ELLIS

What do you expect after what you said about my painting?

DENESCO

What did I say? I said it was a beautiful forgery. That's a compliment.

ELLIS

Damnit, stop talking about forgery. My painting has passed every known test.

DENESCO

I do not doubt it. (*He crosses* ELLIS *to the painting, flips on the light, and surveys it judicially*) Let me see now . . . ah, yes, lovely. You see, Mr. Ellis, a genuine Impressionist canvas was used—perhaps some neglected painter of the period. The original painting was stripped away, perhaps even the surface of the *gesso,* the plaster preparation for the painting. All the paint was prepared from earth and chemicals corresponding to those used in the 19th century and the finished product then aged according to one of several processes. (*He fishes a jewelers loupe from his pocket and examines the painting closely*) Splendid! (*He goes on in the same professorial manner*) You see, at one time it was necessary for the poor forger to simulate age by actually reproducing a pattern of cracks in the surface of the painting. The great Dutch pioneer, Van Meegeren, found a new method which has been invaluable to his followers. The finished painting is covered with a light, highly inflammable varnish and while this substance is still wet the whole surface of the painting is exposed to a quick, high heat. Pft. The varnish burns instantly and harmlessly away. The paint cracks as beautifully and naturally as if it had been hanging in the Louvre for centuries. (*Piously*) We all owe a great debt to Van Meergern for this advance. (*He sighs*) Much as I enjoy these aesthetic matters, I am a man who buys and sells. (*He takes the drawing from tube*) Do me the honor of examining this. You see, it is not only similar to your Reclining Figure—it is identical.

ELLIS

Exactly what the hell is this?

DENESCO

I suggest that is a practice drawing—made by the same genius who did this. You are not looking at it properly, Mr. Ellis—let me show you. The drawing is a masterpiece, isn't it? Every stroke of the pencil imparts the genius of Renoir, doesn't it? (*Holds it to the light*) I hold the drawing to the light. *Voilà*. Amazing, isn't it?

There is the watermark on the paper. A work of pure genius executed by Renoir not later than 1878 and he did it on paper that was made in 1933 in Fall River, Massachusetts.

ELLIS

But why would a forger . . .

DENESCO

Practice, Mr. Ellis. Jascha Heifetz himself doesn't practice as much as a virtuoso forger. He must draw and draw until finally he can duplicate the master's hand with no strain, with absolute freedom. That is the crucial test of a disputed painting, Mr. Ellis. Generally, what follows this test is most unpleasant. Shrill cries from the collector, unsympathetic police, tiresome proceedings in court—perhaps even prison for those most intimately concerned.

ELLIS

You son-of-a-bitch! This painting is sold. The man who's buying it likes it. It has passed every test.

DENESCO

And it will continue to do so.

ELLIS

But that drawing would give it all away, wouldn't it?

DENESCO

Lamentably, yes. The drawing would be conclusive proof that a forger could reproduce the natural hand of Renoir. But you can have complete peace of mind.

ELLIS

For a price?

DENESCO

I am a man who buys and sells.

ELLIS

How much?

DENESCO

My brother and I—my brother also buys and sells—we think this worth ten thousand dollars.

ELLIS

For a Renoir drawing?

DENESCO

For a *forgery* of a Renoir drawing. (*He lets this sink in*) It is only a part of your own profit, Mr. Ellis. He need never know.

ELLIS

How many of these little daisies do you have?

DENESCO

Only one. *This* one. (ELLIS *hesitates*) I give you my word of honor.

ELLIS

As a Lieutenant-Colonel in the Royal Roumanian Cavalry?

DENESCO

The field of ethics, Mr. Ellis, is a wide one. I have identified myself as a man who buys and sells. I have not asked for your credentials.

ELLIS

I haven't got ten thousand dollars.

DENESCO

You will have. It is of no importance at the moment.

ELLIS

Credit blackmail!

DENESCO

You can settle with me, if you choose, when your own funds have cleared. I am a member of the Better Business Bureau of Los Angeles.

(*He extends the drawing to* ELLIS.)

ELLIS

You're willing to let me have this—now?

DENESCO

(Putting the drawing into ELLIS' *hand)*
You have an honest face, Mr. Ellis. You will go far.
An honest face, a simple American name—ah, those are
splendid attributes in this business. I—I am a Roumanian—*(Turns away, with a sigh)*—what a handicap! A
legend built on thousands of anecdotes about dishon-
esty invariably precedes me into a room. Most discour-
aging.

ELLIS

One more thing. Who made this forgery?

DENESCO

I'm afraid I can't answer that. I don't know.

ELLIS

How did you get the drawing? I want to know who
did this?

DENESCO

You may, if you please, hand it back to me—and I will
try to find another customer.

ELLIS

You must know who did this.

DENESCO

I say that I do not. I don't see that you have any
course of action but to believe me.

119

ELLIS
(After a moment)

All right. (DENESCO *is instantly all smiles*) But if you turn up with any more of these, I'll kill you. On my word of honor, as a former Staff-Sergeant in the United States Army.

DENESCO

I quite understand, Mr. Ellis. (*Hands him a business card*) I look forward to hearing from you. Good night, Mr. Ellis. (*He starts to go, then turns back*) It was a pleasure doing business with a gentleman.
> (*He goes.* ELLIS *starts quickly for the doors, at left.* WILLIAM *enters, stopping him.*)

WILLIAM

Mr. Ellis, may I speak to you on a personal matter? (ELLIS *nods*) Very few people know this, but I am a painter, a primitive painter.

ELLIS

Oh.

WILLIAM
(Stopping him with a movement)

I started painting late in life. I do scenes of my childhood in the West Indies, not unlike the work of the person who calls herself Grandma Moses, although, with all due modesty, I believe that I am much more primitive.

RECLINING FIGURE

ELLIS

(*This is just what he wanted to hear at the moment*)
I am sure you are, William.

WILLIAM

(*Blocking his path*)
And since you have a gallery specializing in new and unknown painters, and since you are going to become, I believe, a member of our family . . . (ELLIS *gives him a look*) It's true, sir, isn't it—about you and Miss Edgerton?

ELLIS

Well, it may be me and *Mister* Edgerton.

WILLIAM

I don't understand, sir.

ELLIS

Never mind, William. I'll be glad to look at your work.

WILLIAM

Thank you, sir.
(*He goes to the pantry as* CASSY *and* EDGERTON *enter from the vault.*)

CASSY

Oh, you've come down. (*She prods* EDGERTON) Go on—tell him. Nicely.

EDGERTON

How much you asking for the painting?

ELLIS

(*Coldly*)
One hundred thousand dollars.

EDGERTON

Give you a check in the morning.
(AGRAMONTE *comes from the vault, laden with camera, floodlights, and gadget bag.*)

AGRAMONTE

(*Coming downstage on platform*)
My, it's been a long day. Mr. Ellis, I congratulate you! I don't think I've ever tested a painting as thoroughly as I've tested this one, and I've never had such a gratifying response. (*To* EDGERTON) Oh, Mr. Edgerton, our museum is having two distinguished guests tomorrow. May I bring them by to see this?

EDGERTON

I don't want any tourists tracking up the place.

AGRAMONTE

Oh, these aren't tourists. These are distinguished critics and connoisseurs. Top men in their fields.

EDGERTON

Well, all right—if they don't stay too long.

AGRAMONTE

Thank you very much, Mr. Edgerton. Good night . . .
(*He goes out by the terrace doors.*)

CASSY
(*Calling after him*)
Good night.

EDGERTON
(*At the painting*)
There will be a lot of big-shots wanting to see this. I
think I'm going to get a kick out of it. Ellis, you came
up with a good thing here.

ELLIS

Thanks.

EDGERTON

Any time you run across something special like this,
you come to me. Do you hear—come to me.

ELLIS

Yes. Yes, I will, Mr. Edgerton. I'll be glad to. (CASSY
is looking at him, surprised) As a matter of fact, I know
a great buy I can make on a fine Daumier. I saw it in
Paris this trip, but I didn't have the capital. Now, I
could get it for you.

EDGERTON

Good. As long as this is such a fancy dinner party, I'll wash my hands.

(*He goes to pantry.*)

CASSY

What did you mean, you'll pick up a Daumier for him?

ELLIS

What have you got against Daumier?

CASSY

What's wrong with you? You learn the painting is sold, and you don't react; now you're talking about doing business with my father.

ELLIS

Well, your father is a good customer . . .

CASSY

But what about your own gallery . . . ?

ELLIS

Having a gallery of my own doesn't mean I have to pass up an important deal that comes my way.

CASSY

Sam, listen to me . . .

ELLIS

What are you doing—testing me again? Well, don't bother. I've just tested myself and I've discovered that my character would never measure up to your high parole-board standards.

CASSY

But you told me you had an ideal, and a plan, and you were going to stick to it.

ELLIS

I told you that?

CASSY

Yes.

ELLIS

Well, that's an art dealer for you.
   (WILLIAM *enters from pantry.*)

WILLIAM

Dinner is ready.

CASSY

It ought to be quite a dinner!
   (*She goes, as* EDGERTON *enters from pantry.*)

EDGERTON

Come on, Ellis, let's eat. William, bring that painting into the dining room. I want to look at it all through dinner.
   (*He goes.*)

RECLINING FIGURE

WILLIAM

(Taking painting from easel)

It's so beautiful. I wonder if I've started too late in life to ever accomplish work like this.

ELLIS

You want to paint like this, William? Perseverance! Look at Renoir. In his youth, he worked in a china factory and painted all night. In middle-age, he painted, painted, painted. When he was old and sick, he painted with a brush strapped to his hand. Then in 1919 he died. And even *that* didn't stop him. He kept right on painting!

(He goes out quickly.)

Curtain

ACT THREE

ACT THREE

The next morning.
ASTORG is reading the paper, leaning against the desk.
On the desk is his breakfast tray, finished. He is having
his first cigar of the day.

ASTORG

Ho-hoh! (*He has found an item that interests him.*
WILLIAM *enters from pantry*) Ho-hoh! (*With sudden de-*
cision, he turns to WILLIAM) William, what time is it
now in Texas?

WILLIAM

Well, sir, it's just before ten o'clock here on the Pacific
Coast. Mountain Time would be one hour later.

ASTORG

Mountain Time? The whole of Texas is as flat as a
schnitzel!

WILLIAM

Nevertheless, sir, Mountain Time is the time zone of
that area.

ASTORG

If you say so; you're the butler. (*He muses*) Eleven o'clock—maybe too early—maybe not. William, suppose you just struck a whole new oil field—could you sleep?
(*He has his hand on the phone.*)

WILLIAM

I doubt it very much, sir.
(*He goes to pantry.*)

ASTORG

(*Dialing Long-Distance*)
Operator. (*He does things in a big way*) Texas, please. (*Listens*) Where? Houston, Texas. Mrs. Sanford P. Crowley. (*Listens momentarily*) You'll find it. Everybody knows Mrs. Crowley. Here is Arcadia 8–9191. (*Listens*) I'll hold, I'll hold. (*The vault bell rings.* ASTORG *is startled, looks at his watch.* WILLIAM *comes back from pantry, quickly pours Scotch into an old-fashioned glass*) The time-lock? So soon?

WILLIAM

Mr. Edgerton set it two hours ahead last night. He wants things ready for those art experts.
(WELDON *bursts in from left, takes the drink that* WILLIAM *is already holding out for him.*)

RECLINING FIGURE

ASTORG

Everything is mixed up. It is only ten o'clock . . .
(*Hastily to the operator*) I'm holding, I'm holding.

WELDON

Ten o'clock! What am I doing with a drink? (*He
drinks anyway*) You know my rule, William. Nothing
before noon.

WILLIAM

I beg your pardon, sir. I thought that was determined
by the bell and not the hour. An automatic response, not
unlike a conditioned reflex.
(*He goes to pantry.*)

ASTORG

You'll start up with him, hah?

WELDON

My idea of really rich is to be able to afford an il-
literate butler.
(*He gets up and goes to bar for a refill.*)

ASTORG

Sure I'm here. Where is Texas? (*Pause*) I'm holding,
I'm holding, darling. (*To* WELDON, *who is starting for
the vault*) A customer in Texas. Weldon, what would
you suggest for an old lady with a new oil field?

WELDON

A pump.

ASTORG

No, no. A painting. I've got to sell her something before Nieman-Marcus gets hold of her.

WELDON

Say, why don't I get out my old paint-box and knock you off a few things.

ASTORG

Oh, wouldn't I love to do that to Texas!

WELDON

Give me two hours and I'll deliver a half-a-dozen white-period Utrillos.

ASTORG

Utrillo! (*He is pained*) For a man of your talent? Everybody fakes Utrillos. It is the fourth biggest industry in France. Now, if it was another great Renoir, that would be different.

WELDON

I can't go on painting Renoirs for the rest of my life.

ASTORG

It was good enough for Renoir.

132

RECLINING FIGURE

WELDON

I refuse to get into a rut!

ASTORG

(*Into the phone*)

Hello! Mrs. Crowley? Here is Astorg. I'm fine. And how is the most gracious lady in the Lone Star State?

WELDON

Ride 'em, Cowboy!
(*He goes into vault.*)

ASTORG

(*Hand on mouthpiece*)

Shhh! (*Into phone*) What? What kind of news? No, I haven't seen the papers this morning. How charming! Another oil-field! Where? On your tennis court? Ah! Well, too much exercise is no good. By a coincidence, I happen to be coming to Houston tomorrow. (*Listens*) No, I didn't intend to do any business, but if I could be of service to you, my dear Mrs. Crowley. (*Then suddenly*) Ah! I have a fantastic idea. You know that spot in your living room, over the fireplace, where you now have that stuffed moose—well, I know of a superb Toulouse-Lautrec. Toulouse-Lautrec. (*Listens*) Yes . . . yes . . . that's it . . . marvelous . . . I agree with you . . . Jose Ferrer was wonderful . . . no, he's not really so short. He wore special shoes . . . I agree with you, he shouldn't have died in the end. I told them . . . Well, *this* is one of his paintings . . . a masterpiece . . . Yes, hand-painted. It's a painting of Jane Avril. That's right, Zsa Zsa Gabor! (CASSY *comes in from left, dressed in riding pants and a shirt*) Mrs. Crowley, I have to go now. I'll see you in Houston tomorrow. (*To* CASSY) Cassy, wait a minute! (*She stops*) No, I wouldn't sell it to anyone else. I'll bring it straight to you. Good-bye, Mrs. Crowley. (*He hangs up*) Texas! (*And to* CASSY) Where are you running, Cassy?

CASSY

I'm going out.

ASTORG

I want to talk to you. The dinner last night was like the last act of *The Cherry Orchard*. You didn't talk. Ellis didn't talk.

CASSY

That's right.

(EDGERTON *appears from bedroom in robe and slippers.*)

EDGERTON

Say, did the vault bell ring? What a sleep I had! Best in years. Cassy! (*She stops in doorway*) Where you going?

CASSY

Out.

RECLINING FIGURE

EDGERTON

Wait a minute.
> (*He comes down the stairs.*)

CASSY

I'd like to go for a ride. There are times when a girl just wants to be alone with her horse.

ASTORG

What happened last night, Cassy?

CASSY

Nothing . . . nothing at all. Just don't bother about the Archduke Rudolf's tea set.

ASTORG

So!

CASSY

So.

EDGERTON
> (*Coming into room*)

Where's Ellis?

ASTORG

Must be dressing.

CASSY

Don't worry. He won't leave until he gets your check. Not him.

EDGERTON

Something wrong? You and Ellis? The last time we talked you were going to carry him off like a Valkyrie.

CASSY

Well, Wotan—it didn't work.

EDGERTON

When did all this happen?

CASSY

Didn't you notice a peculiar silence at dinner?

EDGERTON

Silence? What silence? I talked. I remember telling the whole story of how I founded the Tingle company, and how I fooled those wise-guys in Wall Street who tried to get it away from me. (*To* ASTORG) You heard me talking, didn't you?

ASTORG

Sure.

EDGERTON

So, what's all this about silence?

RECLINING FIGURE

My dear Lucas, it is true that you told once again your charming business anecdotes, which to me, personally, become more delightful every single time you tell them over and over and over again—(EDGERTON *glares at him*)—but the young people—Cassy and Ellis —did not say a word.

EDGERTON

Really? Why not?

CASSY

What can you say to a man who has just turned you down?

EDGERTON

He turned you down? Lucas Edgerton's daughter?

CASSY

Please—you just struck a nerve.

EDGERTON

Well, Cassy, don't start to wilt and stagger around with a lily in your hand. Keep your chin up. Show a little spark.

ASTORG

Lucas, I don't think Cassy is in the mood for one of your singing commercials.

CASSY

Do they take girls in the Foreign Legion?
(*She goes to terrace.*)

EDGERTON

That's what I get for having a daughter. A son would listen to reason. If he didn't, I'd beat his ears off.

ASTORG

Well, Lucas . . . a young girl . . . she feels rejected.

EDGERTON

Why do you suppose he turned her down?

ASTORG

Well, Lucas, these matters are complicated. Years ago, in Vienna, I once went to call on a psychoanalyst—Sigmund Freud. In those days the science was still young—for two dollars you could lie on the couch all day . . . and he told me . . .

EDGERTON

You know what I think . . . He didn't turn her down. She just got sore at him. I think I know why. Well, he's going to be around here a good deal. It'll work itself out.

ASTORG

Oh? Ellis is going to be around here? Cassy told me he wasn't going to work for you.

EDGERTON

I think he's changed his mind. That's probably what made her unhappy. (*Glancing at Astorg*) I don't think it's making you very happy either.

ASTORG

Lucas, all I ask is the privilege of serving you, as in the past, honestly, humbly, faithfully until the Greatest Collector of them all—(*Pointing up*)—calls on my talents for the Final Exhibition.

EDGERTON

You're not even dead yet and you're looking for another client. Astorg, I think this boy, Ellis, is going to be able to look after me.

ASTORG

No, Lucas. You've bought one picture from Ellis. That's enough. The firm of Jonas Astorg & Company will continue to represent you. And you will always be the gem in our collection of collectors.

EDGERTON

I think you're crazy. You've been looking at too many Picassos. Jonas Astorg & Company! I made you! (WEL-

DON *has come from vault, carrying the painting, and is propping it on easel*) Careful with that.

WELDON

I'll treat it as if it were my own.
(*Pours himself a drink.*)

EDGERTON

You can't find things like this while you're chasing all over the country after a bunch of other clients. And that's why we're washed up. I've got to get dressed now. Those people will be arriving to look at the painting.

WELDON

People? Here in Bleak House? People?

ASTORG

Not exactly people—art experts.

EDGERTON

A couple of big shots—museum directors. Agramonte says they want to write articles about this great new Renoir. I've never gone in for that kind of publicity, but with this painting—well, it's the first thing I've owned that I sort of want people to see. (*He shouts into pantry door*) William! Tell Mr. Ellis to come down. I've got his check ready. A hundred thousand—(*Needling* ASTORG) —dollars. (*He goes up the stairs, singing*) Tingle Bells,

Tingle Bells, Tingle all the way. Tingle, Tingle, Tingle, Tingle . . . (*From balcony, as* ASTORG *rises*) Don't be too hard on me, Astorg—remember your Middle-European charm.

(*He goes to bedroom.*)

ASTORG

I tell you . . . I wouldn't even talk to another art dealer the way he talks to me. (*Indicates painting*) Thank God for this. Wait till I tell him.

WELDON

When does the balloon go up?

ASTORG

I must be patient for a few weeks. Wait till the experts see it; wait till they write articles about it. Great Collector Acquires Unknown Masterpiece. And then one day, quietly, I will say, "Lucas, your bluebird of happiness is a turkey."

WELDON

Listen, he's not going to know that we had anything to do with it?

ASTORG

Oh, no. The man who painted this atoned for his sin by dying for the Resistance in Toulon.

RECLINING FIGURE

WELDON

(Saluting)

I did?

ASTORG

Delightful, no? (*He sees* ELLIS *in the hallway*) Paul—
I must say I do not agree with you about Degas. Oh,
hello, Ellis.

ELLIS

Hello. Where's Mr. Edgerton?

ASTORG

In his cage—dressing. Come, Paul. It always pains me
to see another art dealer get paid.
    (*They are near the terrace doors, when* EDGERTON
    appears, still in bathrobe.)

EDGERTON

Here you are, son—your check. (*It is folded like a
paper airplane, and he sails it down*) Don't thank me.
You earned it.
    (ELLIS *stares at it.*)

ASTORG

One time years ago, he put my check in a glass box at
the bottom of the swimming pool, and made me dive for
it.

(ASTORG *and* WELDON *go to terrace.*)
(ELLIS *picks up the check.* WILLIAM *emerges from pantry, takes painting from easel and starts right.*)

WILLIAM

Mr. Edgerton wants the experts to see this in natural light.

ELLIS

What that thing needs is a total eclipse.
(CASSY *enters from terrace.*)

CASSY

(*As* WILLIAM *props painting against the urn*)
William, will you tell Mr. Ellis I would like to . . . (*She sees him*) Never mind, William. (*He goes*) Good morning, Sam.

ELLIS

Good morning.

CASSY

I went out riding, and suddenly decided to turn back. You know why?

ELLIS
(*Starting out*)

Indians.

CASSY

Where are you going?

ELLIS

Back to New York.

CASSY

Not without me. (*He looks at her, startled*) Thought you got rid of me, didn't you?

ELLIS

Frankly, yes.

CASSY

Ten minutes ago I thought so, too . . . but I've got Scotch tape in my veins.
(*She advances on him.*)

ELLIS

(*Backing off*)
You keep away from me!

CASSY

Sam, I've decided that I like you too much to let you ruin your life by turning down a girl like me. What happened last night?

ELLIS

Nothing happened.

CASSY

Have you got another girl?   .

RECLINING FIGURE

ELLIS

I haven't got any girl. Present company included.

CASSY

Do you have a dread family disease, like the Haps-
burgs? (*He doesn't answer*) Then what . . .

ELLIS

Questions, questions! All right, Miss Bureau of Standards, I'll answer your questions. Maybe I'm fussy but
I don't think it's good form to swindle a man out of a
hundred thousand dollars while I'm holding his daughter on my lap. (*Points to painting*) Last night I found
out that Miss Liberty is a fake. She's as phony as a set of
purple teeth.

CASSY

So that's why . . .

ELLIS

That's why. And don't go running to your father because there's only one way to prove it's a forgery, and I
tore that up.

CASSY

I wouldn't dream of telling him. I couldn't. My father
loves this picture—and with those art experts coming to
see it . . . he'd turn into a mushroom-shaped cloud.
(*Rises*) So it looks as if we're in this together.

ELLIS
(Rises)

Cassy, do me a favor, get back on Trigger and ride off into the golden sunset. I'm a crook. I sold your father the painting after I learned that it was a forgery. I've got his check in my pocket and I'm going to cash it in the morning.

CASSY

Well, we're not really swindling him—we're just obtaining a dowry under false pretenses.

ELLIS
(Protesting)

Cassy, I've got no character at all.

CASSY

Sam, all last night when I was tossing and turning, I realized that it wasn't because of ethics or integrity or ideals . . . *(They kiss, then)* . . . That's what it was. *(They kiss again.)*

ASTORG
(He comes from terrace, surprised)

He has already sold the picture—this must be personal. *(They break apart)* Again it's springtime in Budapest?

CASSY

Astorg, you can dust off Archduke Rudolf's tea set.

ASTORG

So! It's finally going to be something? (*To* ELLIS) And you—you are going to work for Edgerton?

CASSY

(*Firmly, as* ELLIS *opens his mouth*)
No.

ASTORG

What am I talking—tea set? For you I have a fabulous gift. An antique hand-carved four-poster bed which once belonged personally—to Rasputin!

CASSY

I think we'd rather sleep in the tea set.

ELLIS

Let's take the bed and the tea set.

ASTORG

It's a deal.

ELLIS

Now we've got a place to wait while the tea is boiling.

(AGRAMONTE *enters with* DR. HICKEY.)

AGRAMONTE

In here, Dr. Hickey. (HICKEY *is a medium-sized, very aggressive-looking man.* AGRAMONTE *indicates the group*) May I present Dr. Howard Hickey, of the Wildheim Foundation of Cleveland. Miss Edgerton—Dr. Hickey.

HICKEY

How do you do?

CASSY

Nice to have you here.

AGRAMONTE

Mr. Ellis.

HICKEY

You're the big discoverer, eh? (ELLIS *nods*) We'll see.

ASTORG

It isn't necessary to introduce me to Dr. Hickey—we are old friends. How are you, my dear doctor?

HICKEY

Hello, Astorg. Still soaking the rich?

ASTORG

Why should I soak the poor people?

AGRAMONTE

I must help Professor Jumelle in. Excuse me.
(*He goes.*)

148

RECLINING FIGURE

ASTORG

Tell me, where is the lovely Mrs. Hickey?

HICKEY

She's on a field trip. Sumatra jungle. Native sex habits.

ASTORG

Charming! You know, Ellis, Dr. Hickey is a specialist in Impressionist painting.

HICKEY

I am not.

ASTORG

Excuse me—perhaps I should say Post-Impressionist.

HICKEY

You should not.
(HICKEY *puffs unconcernedly during the ensuing pause.*)

CASSY

(*Finally*)
What is your specialty, Dr. Hickey?

HICKEY

My dear young lady, art is art, painting is painting, sculpture is sculpture.

ELLIS

You know, I don't think I've ever heard it put quite that way.

CASSY

Dr. Hickey, I think you and my father will get along beautifully.

ELLIS

Like Rum'n Tingle.

> (EDGERTON *appears from his bedroom, singing "Tingle Bells, Tingle Bells, Tingle All the Way" He comes down the stairs.*)

ASTORG

You know, Hickey, this is not only a treasure house of painting but also of music.

> (EDGERTON *comes into room, dressed immaculately in a cutaway. It is an overpowering effect.*)

EDGERTON

(Very politely)

I didn't realize anyone had arrived. I'm terribly sorry. Do forgive me.

CASSY

(Awed)

I wish *I* had a father like that!

ASTORG

Lucas, I have never seen you looking so well.

EDGERTON

Thank you, Jonas. It isn't every day I have great art experts in the house.

ASTORG

(Dazzled)

Lucas, permit me to introduce Doctor Howard Hickey, of the Wildheim Foundation of Cleveland.

EDGERTON

Mighty happy to know you, Doctor. (*Shaking hands*) I'm very anxious for your opinion of my new Renoir. Agramonte tells me you might do an article on it for the Sunday *Times*.

HICKEY

(Takes pipe out of his mouth)

If it's any good.

(Puts pipe right back.)

EDGERTON

(Smiling, with difficulty)

I think you'll like it. I've read some of your stuff. Very interesting. Of course, I didn't understand a lot of it . . .

HICKEY
(Takes pipe out)
You wouldn't. I try not to write down to the average untutored layman.

EDGERTON
(Seething, quietly)
Average . . . untutored . . . layman . . . (CASSY *puts her fingers in her ears,* ELLIS *bends over, as if avoiding a bomb blast)* Listen, Doctor, you can take your foundation, and the city of Cleveland, and the whole State of Ohio . . .

ASTORG
(Quickly)
How about a drink? Some Hickey, Dr. Tingle?

HICKEY
No, thank you. I'd like to see that painting of yours, Mr. Edgerton.
(EDGERTON nods with difficulty.)

EDGERTON
Yes. Right over here. (*Leads* HICKEY *toward the painting)* Did you come alone?

ELLIS
Mrs. Hickey is in the Sumatra jungle.

EDGERTON

Naturally. (*He and* HICKEY *go up the steps to the painting*) Dr. Hickey, I'd like to point out some things . . .

HICKEY

Mr. Edgerton, I don't like to be spoken to while I'm looking at a painting.

EDGERTON
(*After a slow burn*)

Oh!

(AGRAMONTE *enters, leading the very old* PROFESSOR JUMELLE *a doddering art critic who may possibly be the oldest one in captivity.*)

AGRAMONTE

Par ici, M. le Professeur.

JUMELLE
(*Mumbling*)

Bon . . . bon . . .

AGRAMONTE

May I present Professor Phillipe Jumelle, Société des Arts Nationale de Paris. (*Introducing him*) Monsieur le Professeur . . . Mademoiselle Edgerton.

RECLINING FIGURE

Enchanté, Mademoiselle. *(To* AGRAMONTE) *Très gentille.*

AGRAMONTE

Monsieur Ellis.

JUMELLE

Bonjour, Monsieur.

ELLIS

Bonjour.

AGRAMONTE

Et naturellement vous connaissez Monsieur Astorg?

ASTORG

Bonjour, Jumelle.

JUMELLE

(Peers at ASTORG *a moment, then lets his monocle drop in disgust)*
Ah!

AGRAMONTE

Et maintenant, Monsieur Lucas Edgerton—*le patron.*

EDGERTON

How are you, Professor?

JUMELLE

Enchanté, Monsieur Edgerton.
> (*He turns to* AGRAMONTE *as* EDGERTON *turns to*
> ASTORG.)

EDGERTON

Doesn't he speak any English?

JUMELLE

Est ce qu'il ne parle pas français?

(*Simultaneously.*)

ASTORG

No.

AGRAMONTE

Non.

(*Simultaneously.*)

EDGERTON

Agramonte, you've brought me two experts and I can't talk to either of them.

AGRAMONTE

Mr. Edgerton, we're extremely fortunate in having Professor Jumelle. He actually knew Renoir.

JUMELLE

(*Lighting up at the magic name*)
Ah, Renoir. *J'ai très bien connu* Renoir.

155

RECLINING FIGURE

AGRAMONTE

He is saying how well he knew Renoir.

JUMELLE

Il était comme un oncle pour moi.

AGRAMONTE

Like an uncle to him.

JUMELLE

La grande affection l'un pour l'autre.

AGRAMONTE

They loved each other.

JUMELLE

Ah, ce pauvre Renoir.

AGRAMONTE

Poor Renoir.

JUMELLE

Il est mort.

AGRAMONTE

He is dead.

JUMELLE

C'est la vie.

156

AGRAMONTE

That's life.

EDGERTON

Agramonte, you've come up with a live wire. You hear that, Ellis? We're going to show our painting to a guy who actually knew Renoir.

JUMELLE

(The magic name)

Renoir . . .

AGRAMONTE

He devoted his whole life to the study of Renoir. He knows every single painting—without exception—that Renoir ever executed.

EDGERTON

Tell him that I'd like him to see the rest of the Collection after he looks at this painting.

AGRAMONTE

(Leading JUMELLE *to the painting)*

Monsieur Edgerton *vous prie d'inspecter la collection complète.*

JUMELLE

Bon. Avec le plus grand plaisir. (He prods HICKEY, *who is crouched, examining the painting) Pardon,* Monsieur. (HICKEY *moves upstage to let* JUMELLE *see the painting.* JUMELLE *croons quietly) Ça . . . Ça . . . Ça . . . Ah, le maître . . . ça c'est le meilleur de tout ce que Pierre Auguste a jamais peint en cette période.*

HICKEY

Dans toute sa vie!

EDGERTON

What? What?

AGRAMONTE

They're saying it's the best thing Renoir ever painted.

EDGERTON

You hear that Astorg?

ASTORG

I hear it.

HICKEY

Edgerton, you probably don't deserve it but this is the finest thing of its kind. (*To* ELLIS) Ellis, this is a fascinating discovery. How did it happen?

ELLIS

Oh, let's just say that I stepped into it.

EDGERTON

(*To* CASSY)

What's the matter with him?

RECLINING FIGURE

CASSY

Modesty.

JUMELLE

Renoir *était très fier de cette peinture.*

AGRAMONTE

Renoir was very proud of this.

JUMELLE

Il en parlait souvent pendant notre souper.

AGRAMONTE

They talked about it when they were having supper.

JUMELLE

Nous étions assis là avec une bouteille de vin.

AGRAMONTE

We would sit there over a bottle of wine.

JUMELLE

Probablement une bonne purée.

AGRAMONTE

Probably some soup.

JUMELLE

Un saucisson.

159

AGRAMONTE

Sausage.

JUMELLE

Du fromage.

AGRAMONTE

Cheese.

JUMELLE

Des fruits.

AGRAMONTE

Fruit.

JUMELLE

Du café.

AGRAMONTE

Coffee.

JUMELLE

Pauvre Renoir.

AGRAMONTE

Poor Renoir.

JUMELLE

Il est mort.

AGRAMONTE

He's dead.

RECLINING FIGURE

EDGERTON

I wish he wouldn't keep telling us Renoir was dead.

JUMELLE

*Ce qui me plaît tant c'est que ça nous montre si bien
l'influence de l'école de Barbizon.*

AGRAMONTE

He likes it because it shows the influence of the Barbizon School.

HICKEY

Barbizon School! They painted nothing but sheep.

AGRAMONTE

Dr. Hickey, perhaps you're being hard on the Barbizon painters. What do you think, Mr. Astorg?

ASTORG

As I always say, art is art, painting is painting, sculpture is sculpture.

AGRAMONTE

Very good! Did you hear that, Dr. Hickey?

HICKEY
(Coldly)

He heard it too.

RECLINING FIGURE

JUMELLE

(From his dream world)
Cette jeune fille, ce modèle là, c'était Thérèse Chaux-temps.

AGRAMONTE

He knew the model, Therese Chauxtemps.

JUMELLE

Une très jolie fille.

AGRAMONTE

She was a very pretty girl.

JUMELLE

Thérèse et moi sommes devenus de très bons amis.

AGRAMONTE

He became good friends with the model.

JUMELLE

Vraiment pour quelque temps nous faisions bon ménage ensemble.
(AGRAMONTE *looks pained and shocked.*)

AGRAMONTE

The old rascal! They lived together.

RECLINING FIGURE

ASTORG

No wonder he's such an expert.

(WELDON *appears in the terrace doorway.*)

EDGERTON

There's one question I'd like to ask Professor Jumelle . . . Ask him if he knows where Renoir painted this.

AGRAMONTE

Dans quelle localité est-ce que Renoir *a fait cette peinture?*

JUMELLE

Evidemment en Provence.

AGRAMONTE

In Provence.

HICKEY

Provence? This orchestration of color? Not in Provence. You don't find that light in Provence. Iridescence, yes; evanescence, maybe, incandescence, never. This harmony of light could be produced only near Paris. Those crashing chords of blue—Paris. The subdued lyricism of green—Paris. The poetic play of light on the body of the model! Magnificent study! (*To* EDGERTON) Does it have a title?

EDGERTON

Title—I—I don't know . . .

WELDON

Yes, it has a title. "Renoir's Mother." Excuse me, Doctor—go on with your autopsy.
(*Goes to bar, pours Scotch. There is understandably a moment of shock.*)

ASTORG

(*Hurriedly*)
Perhaps the gentlemen would like to see the rest of the Collection.

EDGERTON

I think that's a good idea. (*He glares at* WELDON. AGRAMONTE *starts taking them to vault*) Gentlemen, I appreciate your comments. Let Agramonte show you the main Collection downstairs.

HICKEY

All right. I'd like to see what you've got buried there.

EDGERTON

You'll enjoy it, I think. Thank you.
(HICKEY *goes into the vault first.*)

JUMELLE

(*As they go*)
Thérèse Chauxtemps aussi est morte.

RECLINING FIGURE

AGRAMONTE

He says Thérèse Chauxtemps is dead, too.

EDGERTON

(*Turning on* WELDON)

Well, so your brilliance finally ran away with you. You couldn't stand hearing a couple of big men praising my picture.

WELDON

The hot air went to my head.

EDGERTON

I know what went to your head—hearing them praise another painter, even if he's dead.

WELDON

They weren't praising *Renoir* . . .

ASTORG

Paul!

WELDON

They were dissecting him.

EDGERTON

What would you know about it? What would you know about anything—except what comes out of a bottle?

RECLINING FIGURE

WELDON

Which reminds me.

(He starts to bar, but EDGERTON *is in the way.)*

EDGERTON

No, you don't. No more whiskey for you in this house.

WELDON

Well, I would say that would make this house unbearable.

EDGERTON

You won't have to bear it any longer. You're through!

CASSY

Now, Father . . .

ASTORG

Lucas, please don't be hasty . . .

EDGERTON

You, too. Pack up and get out, Weldon—and take
your empty bottles.

CASSY

Father, what is this? A few minutes ago you were
Little Lord Fauntleroy.

166

RECLINING FIGURE

WELDON

You're all very kind. But I'll be glad to go. How long can a man be buried in this cemetery of art—run by a glorified soda-jerk?

ASTORG

Paul! Lucas, he's not himself—he loves you.

EDGERTON

No . . . this is the finish. I've put up with his snide Latin Quarter cracks for years. But when he starts making them about my Renoir . . .

WELDON

What makes it your Renoir?

EDGERTON

Because I paid a hundred thousand dollars for it. And let me tell you one more thing . . .

WELDON

I'll tell you one more thing—*I painted it.*
(ELLIS *rises. In the frozen silence,* ASTORG *hums the main part of the "Blue Danube Waltz."*)

EDGERTON

What did you say?

WELDON

I painted that.

EDGERTON

Well, that does it—you've completely lost your mind.

WELDON

You don't think I'm capable of it, do you? Well, I painted it and I want you to know it even if I hang for it.

EDGERTON

I fell I'm dealing with a dangerous maniac. Cassy, call somebody. A hospital . . .

CASSY

I could use one myself.

EDGERTON

Ellis, do you hear what he's saying about your painting?

WELDON

I'm telling you the truth. I forged this in 1937, in Paris. Astorg knows it.

ASTORG

Paul, you're upset. I think he has a fever . . .

WELDON

I did it in your flat, in Montparnasse.

ELLIS

Mr. Edgerton . . .

EDGERTON

Now wait a minute. Everybody be quiet. (*To* WELDON)
You listen to me. I don't want to hear any more about
this. You're a sick man. Go up and lie down—we'll get
you a doctor.

ELLIS

Mr. Edgerton . . .

EDGERTON

(*Goes right on talking to* WELDON)
If you go on talking like this, I'll have you arrested.

WELDON

But I tell you . . .

EDGERTON

Do as you're told—go and lie down—don't let me hear
another word about this.

ELLIS

(*Finally breaking in, sharply*)
Mr. Edgerton. (EDGERTON *turns.* ELLIS *takes the air-
plane shaped check from his pocket, and sails it at* ED-
GERTON'S *feet*) Your check. Making a return flight.

CASSY

He *is* a good boy!

ELLIS

Mr. Edgerton, I'm sorry that the first painting you
ever really cared about had to be a forgery, but it is.

EDGERTON

You're all insane . . . what about Agramonte? . . .
that expert . . . he knew Renoir personally. Are you
trying to tell me that there's any connection between
that idiot—(*Indicates* WELDON)—and this . . .?
(*To the painting.*)

ELLIS

Go on, Weldon, take your bow.

WELDON

Forget it, it was a joke.

ELLIS

Damn it, you're a painter. That's why I'm backing
you. Whatever that is, the man who painted it is an
artist and in my book he's worth twenty dealers, experts
and collectors. Now, get up there.

WELDON

I painted this, as I said, in 1937. (*He goes to painting*)
I was careful about the canvas and the pigments, but

down here, in this lower left hand corner, I deliberately used modern paint. I take it for granted Agramonte found it.

EDGERTON

Yes, he did.

WELDON

I suppose he thought it had been used for retouching. Well, I put it there because that was my signature. If you want any further proof, I'll be glad to draw that foolish look on your face in the natural hand of Renoir.

ELLIS

He can do it, too.

EDGERTON

This is some kind of dealers' trick.

CASSY

Father, Sam is ruining himself by all this—it must be true.

ELLIS

I think I'll be all right, Cassy. I know Mr. Astorg. (*He picks up the painting, and props it up on the sofa*) I know what an ethical man he is. I'm sure he'll want to buy my great Renoir, won't you, Mr. Astorg?

ASTORG

(*To* WELDON)

I didn't think you would expose yourself, but I'm an artistic person. I admire you for it. (*To* ELLIS) Yes, Mr. Ellis, I'll buy the painting—not for myself but as a gift to my dear friend and valued client, Lucas Edgerton.

EDGERTON

Astorg, what are you talking about?

ASTORG

Please, Lucas, I don't like to be spoken to while I'm buying a forgery.

EDGERTON

You knew?

ASTORG

I didn't want to tell him so soon. Lucas, the apple of your eye is a blintz.

EDGERTON

You dirty . . .

ASTORG

No, no, Lucas, if you go on calling me names, then all this was wasted. You see, my dear old friend, you were becoming utterly unbearable. That's why, to save our friendship, I arranged this whole horrible thing. It was an act of love.

EDGERTON

All right. All right. (*To* ASTORG) You're mixed up in this. (*To* ELLIS) You're mixed up in it. (*To* WELDON) You, too. You've confessed. Cassy—get on the phone—call the District Attorney. Tell him I want him over here in five minutes . . . (*Shouting*) Tell him to bring handcuffs for everybody.

CASSY

Father!

ASTORG

Go on, Cassy, phone. It will be a most enjoyable trial. You will have a lovely day on the witness stand.

EDGERTON

Damn right. I'll tell them plenty.

ASTORG

For example?

EDGERTON

(*Hotly*)

I'll tell them that a bunch of cheap crooks—(*He pauses; He's thinking already*)—sold me—(*He pauses*) —Made me look like—made me look like a . . .

(*He realizes his position, sits down abruptly.*)

173

WELDON
(Gently)
Patron, I deem it an honor to hang in your Collection.

EDGERTON
(Bitterly)
Thanks, Renoir. Anybody else want to stick a spear in my carcass while it's still quivering?

CASSY
Father, even if that is a forgery, it started you caring about your paintings, about what other people thought of them, about letting people see them and enjoy them with you. Nothing that was genuine ever moved you that much. Please go on like that, Father.

ELLIS
She's right . . . Dad.

EDGERTON
(Convulsively)
Dad! *(Puts his head in his hands)* That's the end. Ruined by my own personal son-in-law. Go ahead. Go to New York. Live your lives.

CASSY
Father, don't say it that way.

RECLINING FIGURE

EDGERTON

Don't worry about me. I'm all right.

ELLIS

You'd be happier if you'd listen to Cassy. You'd get a lot of pleasure opening the vault—get the pictures up here . . .

EDGERTON

(Suffering)

Anything you say. Open the vault, spread the paintings around. I don't care. I'm finished. You know, when I bought this place, I remember they told me it had been an old Indian burial ground.

ASTORG

Lucas, don't talk like that. You're not an old Indian!
(AGRAMONTE *comes from the vault, followed by* JUMELLE *and then* HICKEY.)

AGRAMONTE

Mr. Edgerton, both my colleagues enjoyed it very much.

JUMELLE

Incroyable! Magnifique! Immense! Je vous remercie, Patron!

AGRAMONTE

He says . . .

EDGERTON

I know—Renoir is dead.

JUMELLE

Oui . . . oui . . . il est mort.
(*He goes to terrace, out with* AGRAMONTE.)

HICKEY

That's quite a collection, Edgerton. Damn shame
you've got it locked up like that.

CASSY

That may all be changed, isn't that so, Father?

ELLIS

Mr. Edgerton is thinking about opening up the Collection to the public.

ASTORG

The Edgerton Collection may even go on tour, like
the Russian ballet.

HICKEY

Well, that's the first sensible thing I've heard today.

EDGERTON

(*A spark of life*)
You like that idea, Doctor?

HICKEY

Very much, Mr. Edgerton.

EDGERTON

(*Fondly*)

You know, I may even move the whole Collection to New York. You see, Doctor, my children will be there and I'd like to be with them.

(ELLIS *reacts, pained.*)

HICKEY

(*Looking at the painting*)

Oh, so New York will have this. It's always that way. They always get the cream.

EDGERTON

(*He rises slowly*)

That *is* great, isn't it, Doctor?

HICKEY

This? In the history of every art, there's one trans-figured moment. Here, in this painting, Renoir stood on the pinnacle, towering over even his own great work.

EDGERTON

It's that good, eh?

HICKEY

Yes!

RECLINING FIGURE

EDGERTON

(Picking up painting, and handing it to HICKEY*)*
Take it. It's yours.

HICKEY

Mr. Edgerton . . .

EDGERTON

Go on, take it. You deserve it.

HICKEY

But, I can't believe it . . . Mr. Edgerton . . . *(Starts a speech.* EDGERTON *relieves him of his pipe)* On behalf of myself . . . the Foundation . . . *(Turning front)* We'll put this in a special room with a bronze plaque. It will say, "To the People of Cleveland, From their Benefactor, Mr. Lucas Edgerton . . ."

EDGERTON

No, No. Nothing like that. Just let it say, "To the Public, From a Friend. With Love."

Curtain